Slow Cookery

JG PRESS

Delicious Recipes for Your Electric Slow Cooker

No matter how busy you are, the wonderful home-cooked soups, stews, and pot roasts of more leisurely times can be yours again, thanks to the convenience of an electric slow cooker. In this new book, we've served up recipes for over 125 savory and satisfying slow-cooked dishes, from fresh-tasting main-dish soups to sturdy stews to cozy desserts. As you look through each chapter, you'll be impressed at the freedom and variety that crockery cooking has to offer. Experience the robust pleasure of Stout-hearted Beef with Garlic Mashed Potatoes, the elegance of Chicken Breasts Calvados, the creamy goodness of Nordic Potato Soup with Ham. Delight vegetarian friends and family members with unhurried Spicy Black Bean Chili or wholesome Pasta with Lentils & Chard. For casual parties, you'll enjoy our saucy sandwich fillings—and you may want to buy a small 2- or 4-cup slow cooker just to try our irresistible hot dips and spreads.

For our recipes, we provide a nutritional analysis (see page 5) prepared by Hill Nutrition Associates, Inc., of Florida. We are grateful to Lynne Hill, R. D., for her advice and expertise. We thank Rebecca LaBrum for editing the mansucript. We also thank Beaver Brothers Antiques, Fillamento, Forrest Jones, and RH for the accessories used in our photographs.

o

Copyright © 2004 World Publications Group, Inc.

World Publications Group
455 Somerset Avenue
North Dighton, MA 02764
www.wrldpub.net

Copyright under International, Pan American, and Universal Copyright Conventions. All rights reserved. No part of this book may be reproduced or transmitted in any form or by any means, electronic or mechanical, including photocopying, recording, or any information storage-and-retrieval system, without written permission from the copyright holder. Brief passages (not to exceed 1,000 words) may be quoted for reviews.

ISBN 1-57215-391-1

Research and text: Cynthia Scheer
Coordinating Editor: Lynda J. Selden
Cover design: Lynne Yeamans
Design and illustration: Susan Sempere
Photographer: Kevin Sanchez
Photo Stylist: Susan Massey-Weil

Printed and bound in China by SNP Leefung Printers Limited
1 2 3 4 5   06 05 04 03 02

Contents

Snappy Meatball Heroes (recipe on page 29), winning football-watching fare from the slow cooker

Special Features

SLOW DOWN & SAVE TIME

This is an age when everyone seems busier than ever, and time is precious. Yet paradoxically, a Crock-Pot® slow cooker* or any other electric slow cooker—devices designed to prolong cooking time—can help you win valuable minutes when you need them most: at the end of a long, hard day.

As countless satisfied users can attest, you can quickly fill your slow cooker with meat, chicken, or other favorite foods in the morning, then be greeted hours later by the enticing aroma of a savory dinner dish that's almost ready to serve.

The Electric Slow Cooker

At the heart of most (though not all) slow cookers is a ceramic or crockery container. Many newer models offer the advantage of removable cooking inserts; besides being easier to clean than fixed

containers, these are convenient for serving, since they can be lifted out and brought straight to the table.

The electric coils providing the heat for cooking are embedded in a metal sheath that surrounds (or, in some cases, lies beneath) the ceramic container. To set the heat level, you use a dial on the outside of the cooker. Like most other small appliances, a slow cooker can be plugged into virtually any standard household electrical outlet.

Standard slow cookers range in capacity from 3 to 6 quarts; you'll also find "mini-pots" that hold just 2 or 4 cups (these are ideal for hot dips; see pages 84 and 85). In our recipes, we generally state the minimum size appropriate for each dish; for example, you may be directed to use a "4-quart or larger" cooker. If your cooker is below the suggested size, you may not have adequate room for

*Crock-Pot® slow cooker is a registered trademark of The Rival Company.

all the ingredients. Nor should you use too large a cooker; for best results, most manufacturers recommend that the pot be at least half full.

How to Cook Slowly

Most slow cookers offer two heat settings: *low* and *high*. Once the cooker's contents reach the maximum *low* heat, the food temperature remains just below the boiling point; at the *high* setting, food bubbles gently and cooks approximately twice as fast as at low heat. **If your cooker's settings differ from those just described (some models offer more than two choices), consult the manufacturer's instructions to determine the levels corresponding to *low* and *high*.**

At the low setting (used in most of our recipes), foods simmer so gently that natural variations in cooking time are exaggerated. That is, the slightly tougher piece of meat or larger potato chunk that requires an extra 15 minutes on the rangetop may need another hour in a slow cooker—a fact reflected in the fairly wide cooking ranges we state at the start of each recipe. Obviously, you don't need to fret about split-second timing: if you arrive home half an hour later than expected, your pot roast, stew, or crock of beans is unlikely to be ruined.

Most of our recipes can be assembled in a minimum of time, allowing a speedy getaway in the morning. If your cooker has a removable insert, you can manage your time in the kitchen especially conveniently: just prepare your ingredients and combine them in the insert in advance, then cover and refrigerate. The next day, you can simply place the insert back in the electric unit to begin cooking.

What's Different about Cooking So Slowly?

Whenever your slow cooker is in use, the tight-fitting cover should be in place; so little heat is produced that you don't want any of it to escape. Even too much lid-lifting for peeking and tasting will prolong the cooking time. It's best just to leave the pot unwatched and relax until the dish is almost done.

Because there's only minor evaporation from a slow cooker, most of our recipes start with a minimum of liquid. The vegetables, meats, or poultry in each dish release additional moisture as they simmer, eventually producing a flavorful broth that can form the base for a savory sauce or gravy (we often stir in cornstarch or other thickening as a final step).

The subtle heat of a slow cooker is especially effective in making less tender cuts of meat juicy and succulent. Surprisingly, even a sizable pot roast becomes fork-tender in less time than is needed to slow-cook a whole carrot or potato. For this reason, our recipes generally instruct you to finely chop or thinly slice vegetables, ensuring that every ingredient will be uniformly cooked.

If you live in a high-altitude area and typically extend conventional cooking times correspondingly, you may find that your slow-cooker times are also longer than those our recipes specify.

In slow cooking, you'll use little if any fat. Meats and other foods rarely need to be browned in oil or butter before they go into the cooker, though we've occasionally found it useful to pan- or oven-brown large cuts of meat to eliminate some of their fat. When fat is exuded by meat or poultry during slow-cooking, be sure to skim it from the cooking liquid before completing and serving the dish.

Planning Slow-cooked Meals

Aside from one chapter of accompaniments (pages 79 through 93), this book offers largely main-dish recipes that require only a crisp green salad, hot rice or potatoes, and a warm loaf of crusty bread to make a satisfying meal. On occasion, you may want to add a fresh vegetable, steaming hot from the microwave, for a tender-crisp finishing touch. Judiciously employed, slow cooking can produce the fastest food you've ever served!

A Word about Our Nutritional Data

For our recipes, we provide a nutritional analysis stating calorie count and percent of calories from fat; grams of protein, carbohydrates, total fat, and saturated fat; and milligrams of cholesterol and sodium. Generally, the analysis applies to a single serving, based on the number of servings given for each recipe and the amount of each ingredient. If a range is given for the number of servings and/or the amount of an ingredient, the analysis is based on an average of the figures given.

The nutritional analysis does not include optional ingredients or those for which no specific amount is stated. If an ingredient is listed with a substitution, the information was calculated using the first choice.

*Dill-flecked Nordic Potato Soup with Ham (recipe on page 9) makes a hearty
supper with crusty rye bread, a salad of marinated sliced cucumbers and
red onions, and a foamy mug of dark beer.*

SIMMERED SOUPS

Unhurried and unattended, soups simmer to perfection in a slow cooker.

Before you rush off to tend to the day's concerns, take a few minutes to fill the

cooker with vegetables, herbs, broth, and—if you choose—some meat or chicken

for added substance. Hours later, you can savor the transformation time has

brought about: a tantalizing soup for a light supper or even a hearty full meal.

○

Mushroom, Barley & Parsley Chowder

Preparation time: About 25 minutes
Cooking time: 6 to 7 hours

The cooking of Hungary provides the inspiration for this first-course vegetable soup, rich with the color, flavor, and aroma of paprika.

- 1 pound mushrooms, thinly sliced
- 1 clove garlic, minced or pressed
- 1 medium-size onion, finely chopped
- 2 tablespoons sweet Hungarian paprika
- 1 can (about 14½ oz.) pear-shaped tomatoes
- 1 can (about 14½ oz.) beef broth
- ½ cup water
- ½ cup pearl barley, rinsed and drained
- 1 tablespoon red wine vinegar
- ½ cup finely chopped parsley
  Salt and pepper

In a 3-quart or larger electric slow cooker, combine mushrooms, garlic, and onion. Sprinkle with paprika. Cut up tomatoes; add tomatoes and their liquid, broth, water, barley, and vinegar to cooker. Cover and cook at low setting until barley is very tender to bite (6 to 7 hours).

Stir parsley into soup; season to taste with salt and pepper. Makes 4 to 6 servings.

Per serving: 134 calories (10% from fat), 6 g protein, 27 g carbohydrates, 2 g total fat (0.2 g saturated), 0 mg cholesterol, 443 mg sodium

Costa Rican Beef & Vegetable Soup with Yellow Rice

Preparation time: About 25 minutes
Cooking time: About 8¼ hours

Lots of lean beef chunks and a full day of cooking contribute to this soup's hearty flavor. Just before dinner time, prepare the rice and add cabbage, fresh corn, and cilantro to the simmering soup.

- 2 pounds lean boneless beef chuck, trimmed of fat and cut into 1½-inch cubes
- 1 large onion, thinly sliced
- 1 cup thinly sliced celery
- 3 cloves garlic, minced or pressed
- 1 dry bay leaf
- 1 large red bell pepper, seeded and cut into thin, bite-size strips
- 1½ cups water
- 2 cans (about 14½ oz. *each*) beef broth
  Yellow Rice (recipe follows)
- 1 large ear corn, cut into ¾-inch-thick slices
- 4 cups coarsely shredded cabbage
- ⅓ cup lightly packed cilantro leaves
  Salt and pepper

Arrange beef cubes slightly apart in a single layer in a shallow baking pan. Bake in a 500° oven until well browned (about 20 minutes). Meanwhile, in a 3½-quart or larger electric slow cooker, combine onion, celery, garlic, bay leaf, and bell pepper.

Transfer browned beef cubes to cooker. Pour a little of the water into baking pan, stirring to dissolve drippings; then pour into cooker. Add broth and remaining water. Cover and cook at low setting until beef is very tender when pierced (about 8 hours).

About 15 minutes before beef is done, prepare Yellow Rice. While rice is cooking, increase cooker heat setting to high; add corn. Cover; cook for 5 more minutes. Add cabbage; cover and cook until cabbage is bright green and both cabbage and corn are tender to bite (8 to 10 more minutes). Stir in cilantro; season to taste with salt and pepper.

Ladle soup into wide, shallow bowls; add a scoop of Yellow Rice to each. Makes 6 servings.

Yellow Rice. Heat 1 tablespoon **salad oil** in a 2-quart pan over medium heat. Add 1 small **onion,** finely chopped; cook, stirring, until onion is soft but not browned (3 to 5 minutes). Stir in 1 cup **long-grain white rice** and ¼ teaspoon **ground turmeric;** cook, stirring occasionally, for about 1 minute. Pour in 1¾ cups **water;** reduce heat to low, cover, and cook until rice is tender to bite (about 20 minutes).

Per serving: 421 calories (32% from fat), 35 g protein, 36 g carbohydrates, 15 g total fat (5 g saturated), 98 mg cholesterol, 649 mg sodium

Pictured on page 6

Nordic Potato Soup with Ham

Preparation time: About 15 minutes
Cooking time: 8 to 8½ hours

Small bowls of this creamy potato soup make an inviting first course. Offer more generous servings as a casual supper entrée, perhaps with crusty rye or other whole-grain bread and a marinated cucumber salad.

- 3 medium-size thin-skinned potatoes (about 1½ lbs. *total*), peeled and diced
- 1 large onion, finely chopped
- 1 smoked ham hock (about 1 lb.)
- 1 tablespoon dry dill weed
- 2 teaspoons grated lemon peel
- ¼ teaspoon ground white pepper
- 2½ cups chicken broth
- 1 tablespoon cornstarch
- ½ cup whipping cream
  Dill sprigs (optional)

In a 3-quart or larger electric slow cooker, combine potatoes, onion, ham hock, dill weed, lemon peel, white pepper, and broth. Cover and cook at low setting until ham hock and potatoes are very tender when pierced (7½ to 8 hours).

Lift out ham hock and let stand until cool enough to handle. Meanwhile, remove about 1 cup of the potatoes with a little of the broth; whirl in a blender or food processor until puréed. Return purée to cooker.

In a small bowl, mix cornstarch and cream; blend into potato mixture. Increase cooker heat setting to high. Remove and discard fat and bone from ham; tear meat into bite-size pieces and stir into soup. Cover and cook, stirring 2 or 3 times, for 20 more minutes. Garnish with dill sprigs, if desired. Makes 4 to 6 servings.

Per serving: 241 calories (37% from fat), 11 g protein, 28 g carbohydrates, 10 g total fat (5 g saturated), 41 mg cholesterol, 941 mg sodium

Lentil Soup with Knackwurst

Preparation time: About 20 minutes
Cooking time: 8 to 8½ hours

Fortifying lentil-and-sausage soups are great favorites throughout Germany and Austria. Try serving this main-dish version with an American classic—flaky baking powder biscuits.

- 1 pound lentils, rinsed and drained
- 2 medium-size onions, finely chopped
- 2 medium-size carrots, finely chopped
- 1 medium-size red bell pepper, seeded and finely chopped
- 2 cloves garlic, minced or pressed
- 1 small dried hot red chile, crushed
- 1 teaspoon dry rosemary
- ¼ teaspoon pepper
- 2 cans (about 14½ oz. *each*) beef broth
- 3 cups water
- 1 can (about 8 oz.) tomato sauce
- 1 pound knackwurst or kielbasa, cut into ½-inch-thick slices
- 2 tablespoons red wine vinegar

In a 3½-quart or larger electric slow cooker, combine lentils, onions, carrots, bell pepper, garlic, chile, rosemary, pepper, broth, and water. Cover and cook at low setting until lentils are very tender when mashed with a fork (7½ to 8 hours).

Remove 2 cups of the lentil mixture and whirl in a blender or food processor until puréed. Return purée to cooker. Increase heat setting to high and add tomato sauce and knackwurst; cover and cook until sausage is heated through (about 30 more minutes). Stir in vinegar. Makes 6 to 8 servings.

Per serving: 463 calories (37% from fat), 28 g protein, 46 g carbohydrates, 19 g total fat (7 g saturated), 38 mg cholesterol, 1,294 mg sodium

Chicken & Rice Soup with Chipotle Chiles

Preparation time: About 15 minutes

Cooking time: 7 to 7½ hours

Fiery, smoky-tasting chipotle chiles season this distinctive soup with the flavors of Oaxaca, a state in Southern Mexico. Look for the chiles in Mexican markets; they're sold both dried and canned (in *adobo* or *adobado* sauce or *en escabeche*). A squeeze of lime juice tempers the soup's heat.

1½	pounds (about 4 large) chicken thighs
1	medium-size onion, finely chopped
2	large carrots, thinly sliced
1	dried or canned chipotle chile
1	teaspoon dry oregano
1	clove garlic, minced or pressed
2	cans (about 14½ oz. *each*) chicken broth
1	cup water
½	cup long-grain white rice
	Salt
¼	cup lightly packed cilantro leaves
	Lime wedges

Rinse chicken, pat dry, and set aside. In a 3½-quart or larger electric slow cooker, combine onion, carrots, chile, oregano, and garlic. Place chicken on top of vegetables; pour in broth and water. Cover and cook at low setting until chicken and carrots are very tender when pierced (6½ to 7 hours).

Lift out chicken and let stand until cool enough to handle. Meanwhile, skim and discard fat from broth mixture; if desired, remove and discard chile. Add rice to broth mixture. Increase cooker heat setting to high; cover and cook until rice is tender to bite (25 to 30 more minutes).

Remove and discard bones and skin from chicken; tear meat into bite-size shreds. Return chicken to soup, cover, and cook until heated through (about 5 minutes). Season soup to taste with salt; stir in cilantro. Offer lime wedges to squeeze into soup to taste. Makes 4 servings.

Per serving: 267 calories (20% from fat), 25 g protein, 28 g carbohydrates, 6 g total fat (1 g saturated), 81 mg cholesterol, 999 mg sodium

Pictured on facing page

Chicken Corn Soup

Preparation time: About 25 minutes

Cooking time: 8 to 8½ hours

Canned cream-style corn gives this substantial but simple-to-prepare soup richness, body, and a touch of sweetness.

1	chicken (3 to 3½ lbs.), cut up
1	large onion, finely chopped
2	medium-size carrots, finely chopped
3	stalks celery, finely chopped
1	medium-size russet potato (about 8 oz.), peeled and diced
¼	cup chopped parsley
¼	cup canned tomato sauce
2	cans (about 14½ oz. *each*) chicken broth
1	can (about 17 oz.) cream-style corn
2	medium-size zucchini (about 8 oz. *total*), cut lengthwise into quarters, then thinly sliced
	Salt and pepper

Rinse chicken, pat dry, and set aside. In a 4-quart or larger electric slow cooker, combine onion, carrots, celery, potato, and 3 tablespoons of the parsley. Add chicken, then pour in tomato sauce and broth. Cover and cook at low setting until chicken and potato are very tender when pierced (7½ to 8 hours).

Lift out chicken and let stand until cool enough to handle. Meanwhile, skim and discard fat from broth mixture. Stir corn into broth mixture; increase cooker heat setting to high. Cover and cook for 15 more minutes.

Remove and discard bones and skin from chicken; tear meat into bite-size shreds. Add chicken and zucchini to soup; cover and cook until zucchini is just tender to bite (10 to 15 more minutes). Season soup to taste with salt and pepper. Sprinkle with remaining 1 tablespoon parsley. Makes 6 to 8 servings.

Per serving: 235 calories (16% from fat), 26 g protein, 24 g carbohydrates, 4 g total fat (1 g saturated), 71 mg cholesterol, 865 mg sodium

Vegetables in abundance enrich Chicken Corn Soup (recipe on facing page). Serve it straight from the slow cooker for a satisfying and nourishing full meal.

MULTICOLORED CHILI

Part soup, part stew, and always thick and rich, chili is a popular main dish. The customary color is, of course, red. For those who favor this traditional look, we offer two red chilis—one a Southwestern-seasoned version with kidney beans, the other a hearty all-meat interpretation (spoon this one into warm tortillas or over fluffy rice, if you like). For a change of color and flavor, try our distinctive black bean chili; or use white beans, green chiles, and turkey in a dish that makes up in flavor what it lacks in pigmentation.

Because a slow cooker simmers so gently, cooking dried beans for chili can take too long to be practical. To hasten the process, we start with quick-soaked beans—boiled briefly, then left to stand in the cooking water for an hour. And since beans cook to tenderness more slowly when combined with acidic foods and liquids (tomatoes, molasses, or wine, for example), we add such foods only when the beans are nearly done. We also use a touch of baking soda to balance the acid content of other ingredients.

New Mexican Red Bean Chili

Preparation time: About 1 hour (including standing time)

Cooking time: 9 to 10½ hours

1 pound dried red kidney beans
2 quarts water
1 large red onion, finely chopped
2 cloves garlic, minced or pressed
2 jars (about 7 oz. *each*) roasted red peppers or pimentos, drained and chopped
1 teaspoon ground allspice
2 teaspoons *each* ground cumin and ground coriander
1½ teaspoons dry oregano
¼ teaspoon baking soda
⅓ cup ground dried New Mexico or California chiles
1½ pounds extra-lean ground beef
2 cans (about 14½ oz. *each*) beef broth
1 can (about 14½ oz.) diced tomatoes
Salt

Rinse and sort through beans. In a deep 3½- to 4-quart pan, bring water to a boil over high heat. Add beans. Let water return to a boil; then boil, uncovered, for 2 minutes. Remove pan from heat, cover, and let stand for 1 hour. Drain and rinse beans, discarding cooking water.

While beans are standing, in a 4-quart or larger electric slow cooker, combine onion, garlic, red peppers, allspice, cumin, coriander, oregano, baking soda, and chiles. Crumble in beef; mix to coat with seasonings. Stir

in beans; pour in broth. Cover; cook at low setting until beans are very tender to bite (8½ to 10 hours).

Increase cooker heat setting to high and stir in tomatoes. Cover and cook until chili is very hot (about 30 more minutes). Skim and discard fat from chili, if necessary. Season to taste with salt. Makes 6 to 8 servings.

Per serving: 508 calories (33% from fat), 37 g protein, 50 g carbohydrates, 19 g total fat (7 g saturated), 67 mg cholesterol, 650 mg sodium

All-meat Red Chili

Preparation time: About 25 minutes

Cooking time: 7 to 8 hours

4 pounds lean boneless beef chuck, trimmed of fat and cut into ¾-inch cubes
6 tablespoons all-purpose flour
1 large onion, finely chopped
4 cloves garlic, minced or pressed
1 large tomato, peeled, seeded, and chopped
1 or 2 canned or pickled jalapeño chiles, seeded and chopped
2 teaspoons dry oregano
1 teaspoon coarsely ground pepper
1½ tablespoons ground cumin
1 tablespoon paprika
3 to 4 tablespoons ground dried pasilla or New Mexico chiles
1 large can (about 15 oz.) tomato sauce
1 cup beer
Salt

Coat beef cubes with flour; shake off excess. In a 3½-quart or larger electric slow cooker, combine beef, onion, garlic, tomato, jalapeño chiles, oregano, pepper, cumin, paprika, and ground chiles; pour in tomato sauce and beer. Cover and cook at low setting until beef is very tender when pierced (7 to 8 hours), stirring once or twice during last 1 to 2 hours of cooking. Skim and discard fat from chili, if necessary. Season to taste with salt. Makes 10 to 12 servings.

Per serving: 266 calories (27% from fat), 37 g protein, 11 g carbohydrates, 8 g total fat (3 g saturated), 99 mg cholesterol, 379 mg sodium

Mellow Black Bean Chili

Preparation time: About 1 hour (including standing time)

Cooking time: 10½ to 12½ hours

1 **pound dried black beans**
2 **quarts plus 1 cup water**
3 **large onions, thinly sliced**
4 **cloves garlic, minced or pressed**
3 **stalks celery, finely chopped**
1 **tablespoon ground cumin**
¼ **teaspoon baking soda**
1 **large can (about 7 oz.) diced green chiles**
2 **cans (about 14½ oz. *each*) chicken broth**
⅓ **cup dry sherry**
3 **tablespoons lemon juice**
1 **to 1¼ pounds kielbasa, thinly sliced**
   Sour cream or plain yogurt
   Prepared chile salsa

Rinse and sort through beans. In a deep 3½- to 4-quart pan, bring 2 quarts of the water to a boil over high heat. Add beans. Let water return to a boil; then boil, uncovered, for 2 minutes. Remove pan from heat, cover, and let stand for 1 hour. Drain and rinse beans, discarding cooking water.

While beans are standing, in a 4-quart or larger electric slow cooker, combine onions, garlic, celery, cumin, baking soda, and chiles. Add beans to slow cooker; pour in broth and remaining 1 cup water. Cover and cook at low setting until beans are very tender to bite (10 to 12 hours).

Remove about 2 cups of the bean mixture and whirl in a blender or food processor until puréed. Return purée to cooker. Increase heat setting to high and stir in sherry, lemon juice, and kielbasa. Cover and cook until sausage is heated through (about 30 more minutes). Serve chili with sour cream and salsa to add to taste. Makes 6 to 8 servings.

Per serving: 520 calories (38% from fat), 27 g protein, 53 g carbohydrates, 22 g total fat (8 g saturated), 49 mg cholesterol, 1,525 mg sodium

White Bean Turkey Chili

Preparation time: About 1 hour (including standing time)

Cooking time: 10 to 10½ hours

1 **pound dried small white beans**
2 **quarts water**
2 **medium-size onions, finely chopped**
4 **cloves garlic, minced or pressed**
1 **large can (about 7 oz.) diced green chiles**
1 **tablespoon ground cumin**
1½ **teaspoons dry oregano**
1 **teaspoon ground red pepper (cayenne)**
½ **teaspoon ground cloves**
¼ **teaspoon baking soda**
2 **turkey thighs (3 to 3½ lbs. *total*), skinned**
3 **cups chicken broth**
½ **cup lightly packed cilantro leaves**
   Salt
   Sour cream (optional)
   Shredded jack cheese (optional)

Rinse and sort through beans. In a deep 3½- to 4-quart pan, bring water to a boil over high heat. Add beans. Let water return to a boil; then boil, uncovered, for 2 minutes. Remove pan from heat, cover, and let stand for 1 hour. Drain and rinse beans, discarding cooking water.

While beans are standing, in a 4-quart or larger electric slow cooker, combine onions, garlic, chiles, cumin, oregano, red pepper, cloves, and baking soda. Rinse turkey, pat dry, and place on top of onion mixture. Add beans to slow cooker; then pour in broth. Cover and cook at low setting until beans are very tender to bite and turkey pulls away from bones in tender shreds (9½ to 10 hours).

Remove turkey and let stand until cool enough to handle. Meanwhile, skim and discard fat from bean mixture, if necessary. Remove 2 cups of the bean mixture and whirl in a blender or food processor until puréed. Return purée to cooker. Increase heat setting to high.

Remove and discard bones and fat from turkey; tear meat into large chunks and return to bean mixture. Cover and cook until turkey is heated through (about 20 more minutes). Stir in cilantro; season to taste with salt. Serve chili with sour cream and cheese to add to taste, if desired. Makes 6 to 8 servings.

Per serving: 400 calories (15% from fat), 40 g protein, 46 g carbohydrates, 7 g total fat (2 g saturated), 90 mg cholesterol, 732 mg sodium

*Fluffy Garlic Mashed Potatoes complement richly flavored, deep brown
Stout-hearted Beef (recipe on page 17). Round out a robust repast
with steamed broccoli spears and a crouton-topped green salad.*

BEEF, LAMB & PORK

For old-fashioned, long-simmered succulence, you can't improve on meat dishes from the slow cooker. With a minimum of effort and attention from you, your crockery cooker turns out juicy pot roasts and stews—and even beef short ribs with authentic barbecue flavor. It helps you cook economically, too: with gentle heat, less costly cuts of beef, lamb, pork, and veal turn meltingly tender.

Slow-cooker Daube of Beef

Preparation time: About 30 minutes
Cooking time: 8 ½ to 9 ½ hours

Traditionally made in a deep pottery casserole, the rich French beef stew known as *daube* translates nicely to a slow cooker. This version is based on a Christmas Eve specialty of Gascony, in southwestern France.

5 shallots, thinly sliced
4 cloves garlic, minced or pressed
2 medium-size carrots, cut into about ¼-inch-thick slices
⅓ cup chopped baked ham
1 strip orange peel (colored part only), about ½ by 3 inches
1 dry bay leaf
1 lean boneless beef chuck roast (2¾ to 3 lbs.), trimmed of fat and cut into 1½-inch cubes
¼ cup all-purpose flour
¼ teaspoon *each* whole black peppercorns and dry thyme
⅛ teaspoon ground cloves
½ teaspoon dry sage

2 tablespoons balsamic vinegar
¾ cup dry red wine or beef broth
¼ cup brandy (optional)
2 tablespoons all-purpose flour blended with 2 tablespoons butter or margarine (at room temperature)
Salt
Chopped parsley

In a 3-quart or larger electric slow cooker, combine shallots, garlic, carrots, ham, orange peel, and bay leaf. Coat beef cubes with the ¼ cup flour; add to cooker. Sprinkle with peppercorns, thyme, cloves, and sage. Drizzle with vinegar; pour in wine and brandy (if used). Cover; cook at low setting until beef is very tender when pierced (8 to 9 hours).

Remove and discard bay leaf and orange peel from stew, then blend in flour-butter mixture. Increase cooker heat setting to high; cover and cook, stirring 2 or 3 times, until sauce is thickened (about 20 more minutes). Season to taste with salt. Sprinkle with parsley. Makes 8 to 10 servings.

Per serving: 257 calories (34% from fat), 33 g protein, 8 g carbohydrates, 9 g total fat (4 g saturated), 97 mg cholesterol, 211 mg sodium

Ginger-Beef Curry

Preparation time: About 25 minutes
Cooking time: 8 to 9 hours

To season this distinctive curry, pass up ready-made curry powder and mix your own pungent blend of sweet and hot spices.

2 large onions, finely chopped
3 tablespoons grated fresh ginger
6 to 8 cloves garlic, minced or pressed
1 cinnamon stick (about 2 inches long)
1 teaspoon *each* ground turmeric and paprika
2½ to 3 pounds lean boneless beef chuck, trimmed of fat and cut into ½- by 2-inch strips
¼ cup all-purpose flour
2 tablespoons ground cumin
1 tablespoon ground coriander
1 teaspoon ground cardamom
½ teaspoon *each* ground cloves and ground red pepper (cayenne)

¼ teaspoon ground nutmeg
⅓ cup tomato paste
⅔ cup water
Salt
⅓ cup lightly packed cilantro leaves

In a 3-quart or larger electric slow cooker, combine onions, ginger, garlic, cinnamon stick, turmeric, and paprika. Coat beef strips with flour, then add to cooker and sprinkle with cumin, coriander, cardamom, cloves, red pepper, and nutmeg. In a small bowl, mix tomato paste and water; pour into cooker. Cover and cook at low setting until beef is very tender when pierced (8 to 9 hours).

Skim and discard fat from beef mixture, if necessary. Season to taste with salt. Stir in all but about 1 tablespoon of the cilantro; sprinkle reserved cilantro over beef. Makes 8 to 10 servings.

Per serving: 215 calories (22% from fat), 31 g protein, 10 g carbohydrates, 5 g total fat (2 g saturated), 82 mg cholesterol, 174 mg sodium

Stout-hearted Beef with Garlic Mashed Potatoes

Preparation time: About 30 minutes

Cooking time: 8 to 9 hours

Dark, full-bodied stout contributes hearty flavor and rich brown color to this robust stew. Serve it over hot, garlicky mashed potatoes.

- 1 **large onion, thinly sliced**
- 2 **cloves garlic, minced or pressed**
- 4 **medium-size carrots, cut into ¼-inch-thick slanting slices**
- ½ **cup finely chopped parsley**
- 1 **dry bay leaf**
- ½ **cup pitted prunes**
- 2 **to 2½ pounds lean boneless beef chuck, trimmed of fat and cut into 1-inch cubes**
- ¼ **cup all-purpose flour**
- ¼ **teaspoon pepper**
- ¾ **cup stout or dark ale**
  Garlic Mashed Potatoes (recipe follows)
  Salt

In a 3-quart or larger electric slow cooker, combine onion, garlic, carrots, parsley, bay leaf, and prunes.

Coat beef cubes with flour, then add to cooker and sprinkle with pepper. Pour in stout. Cover and cook at low setting until beef is very tender when pierced (8 to 9 hours).

About 30 minutes before beef is done, prepare Garlic Mashed Potatoes. Skim and discard fat from stew, if necessary; season to taste with salt. Serve over Garlic Mashed Potatoes. Makes 6 to 8 servings.

Garlic Mashed Potatoes. Peel 4 large **russet potatoes** (2½ to 3 lbs. *total*); cut lengthwise into quarters and place in a 3½- to 4-quart pan. Add 4 cloves **garlic** (sliced); pour in **water** to cover. Bring to a boil over high heat; reduce heat to medium-high and cook, partially covered, until potatoes are very tender when pierced (about 25 minutes). Drain well, then add 2 teaspoons **butter** or margarine and ⅛ teaspoon **ground white pepper.** Beat with an electric mixer (or mash with a potato masher) until smooth; then mix in 4 to 6 tablespoons **lowfat milk,** beating until mixture has a creamy texture. Season to taste with **salt.**

Per serving: 404 calories (14% from fat), 36 g protein, 48 g carbohydrates, 6 g total fat (2 g saturated), 89 mg cholesterol, 145 mg sodium

Braised Green Chile Beef

Preparation time: About 20 minutes

Cooking time: 8¼ to 9¼ hours

This well-seasoned stew blends red wine, green chiles, and chili powder for a flavor that combines the best of *boeuf bourguignon* and *chile con carne*. Serve it with rice or orzo (rice-shaped pasta).

- 1 **large onion, finely chopped**
- 2 **cloves garlic, minced or pressed**
- 1 **small can (about 4 oz.) diced green chiles**
- 1 **small jar (about 2 oz.) sliced pimentos, drained**
- 2 **to 2½ pounds lean boneless beef chuck, trimmed of fat and cut into 1-inch cubes**
- 3 **tablespoons all-purpose flour**
- 2 **tablespoons chili powder**
- 1 **teaspoon *each* dry oregano and ground cumin**
- ¼ **teaspoon pepper**
- 2 **tablespoons catsup**

- ½ **cup dry red wine or beef broth**
- 1 **tablespoon cornstarch blended with 1 tablespoon cold water**
  Salt
  Chopped parsley

In a 3-quart or larger electric slow cooker, combine onion, garlic, chiles, and pimentos. Coat beef cubes with flour, then add to cooker and sprinkle with chili powder, oregano, cumin, and pepper. In a small bowl, mix catsup and wine; pour over beef. Cover and cook at low setting until beef is very tender when pierced (8 to 9 hours).

Blend cornstarch mixture into stew. Increase cooker heat setting to high; cover and cook, stirring 2 or 3 times, until sauce is thickened (10 to 15 more minutes). Season to taste with salt. Sprinkle with parsley. Makes 6 to 8 servings.

Per serving: 236 calories (27% from fat), 32 g protein, 10 g carbohydrates, 7 g total fat (2 g saturated), 88 mg cholesterol, 273 mg sodium

Beef Brisket with Mushrooms

Preparation time: About 20 minutes
Cooking time: 8¾ to 10¼ hours

Serve this succulent roast and its mushroom-wine sauce with brown rice and steamed carrots.

- 1 center-cut fresh beef brisket (4 to 4½ lbs.), trimmed of fat
- ¾ teaspoon coarsely ground pepper
- 1 tablespoon olive oil
- 1 large onion, thinly sliced
- 3 cloves garlic, minced or pressed
- 1 pound mushrooms, cut into quarters
- 1 tablespoon dry rosemary
- ¾ cup dry red wine
- 1 tablespoon Dijon mustard
- 3 tablespoons cornstarch blended with ¼ cup cold water

Sprinkle brisket on all sides with about ½ teaspoon of the pepper. Heat oil in a wide nonstick frying pan over medium-high heat; add brisket and brown well on both sides. Meanwhile, in a 4-quart or larger electric slow cooker, combine onion, garlic, and mushrooms; sprinkle with rosemary and remaining pepper. Place brisket on top of onion mixture. Mix wine and mustard; pour over brisket. Cover; cook at low setting until brisket is very tender when pierced (8½ to 10 hours).

Lift brisket to a warm platter and keep warm. Skim and discard fat from cooking liquid, if necessary; then blend in cornstarch mixture. Increase cooker heat setting to high; cover and cook, stirring 2 or 3 times, until sauce is thickened (about 15 more minutes).

To serve, slice brisket across the grain. Spoon some of the sauce over brisket; serve remaining sauce in a bowl or pitcher to add to taste. Makes 10 to 12 servings.

Per serving: 302 calories (41% from fat), 37 g protein, 6 g carbohydrates, 13 g total fat (4 g saturated), 108 mg cholesterol, 183 mg sodium

Pictured on facing page

Rolled Brisket in Red Wine

Preparation time: About 20 minutes
Cooking time: 9¾ to 10¼ hours

You might accompany this robust pot roast with Garlic Mashed Potatoes (page 17) or noodles.

- 1 center-cut fresh beef brisket (3½ to 4 lbs.), trimmed of fat
-   Freshly ground pepper
- 1 tablespoon olive oil
- 1 large carrot, finely chopped
- 1 large onion, finely chopped
- 1 large leek (white and pale green parts only), thinly sliced
- 1 dry bay leaf
- 1 tablespoon fresh thyme leaves or 1 teaspoon dry thyme
- 4 cloves garlic, minced or pressed
- 1½ cups dry red wine or beef broth
- 3 tablespoons cornstarch blended with 3 tablespoons cold water
-   Thyme sprigs and tomato slices (optional)

Starting with a short side, roll up brisket compactly, jelly roll style; tie roll securely with string at 1½-inch intervals. Sprinkle all over with pepper. Heat oil in a wide nonstick frying pan over medium-high heat; add brisket and brown well on all sides. Meanwhile, in a 4-quart or larger electric slow cooker, combine carrot, onion, leek, and bay leaf; sprinkle with thyme leaves and garlic. Place brisket on top of vegetables; pour in wine. Cover and cook at low setting until brisket is very tender when pierced (9½ to 10 hours).

Lift brisket to a warm platter and keep warm. Skim and discard fat from cooking liquid, if necessary; then blend in cornstarch mixture. Increase cooker heat setting to high; cover and cook, stirring 2 or 3 times, until sauce is thickened (about 15 more minutes).

To serve, remove and discard strings, then slice brisket across the grain. Spoon some of the sauce over brisket; serve remaining sauce in a bowl or pitcher to add to taste. Garnish with thyme sprigs and tomato, if desired. Makes 8 to 10 servings.

Per serving: 331 calories (39% from fat), 40 g protein, 9 g carbohydrates, 14 g total fat (5 g saturated), 117 mg cholesterol, 160 mg sodium

Lean meat at its finest: Rolled Brisket in Red Wine (recipe on facing page), its savory gravy dotted with minced vegetables, offers juicy succulence to match its rich flavor.

Fruited Corned Beef

Preparation time: About 25 minutes

Cooking time: 8 to 10 hours

Baking time: 30 to 40 minutes

Here's a favorite recipe that takes well to slow cooking. After simmering the brisket, you top it with a citrusy sweet-tart crust, then brown it in the oven.

 1 **corned beef brisket (3 to 4 lbs.)**
 1 **small onion, sliced**
 1 **strip orange peel (colored part only), about ½ by 3 inches**
 1 **tablespoon mixed pickling spices**
   Citrus Crust (recipe follows)
 ½ **teaspoon whole cloves**
 1 **tablespoon** *each* **orange juice and lemon juice**
 ¼ **cup apple cider or apple juice**

To remove excess salt from brisket, rinse brisket and place it in a deep 5½- to 6-quart pan; add water to cover. Bring to a boil over high heat, then reduce heat and simmer for 5 minutes; drain. Repeat this step once more.

Meanwhile, in a 4-quart or larger electric slow cooker, combine onion, orange peel, and pickling spices. Place drained brisket on top of onion mixture; pour in 4 cups water. Cover and cook at low setting until brisket is very tender when pierced (8 to 10 hours).

Prepare Citrus Crust. Lift brisket from cooker; place, fat side up, on a rack in a shallow roasting pan. Discard liquid and seasonings in cooker. Stud top of brisket with cloves; pat Citrus Crust over top. Mix orange juice, lemon juice, and cider; drizzle over brisket. Bake in a 375° oven until topping is browned (30 to 40 minutes).

To serve, lift brisket to a warm platter and slice across the grain. Makes 8 to 10 servings.

Citrus Crust. In a small bowl, mix ⅓ cup firmly packed **brown sugar**, 2 tablespoons **fine dry bread crumbs**, 1 teaspoon *each* **dry mustard** and **grated lemon peel**, and 1 tablespoon **grated orange peel**.

Per serving: 357 calories (61% from fat), 23 g protein, 11 g carbohydrates, 24 g total fat (8 g saturated), 122 mg cholesterol, 1,427 mg sodium

Smoky Short Ribs in Red Sauce

Preparation time: About 30 minutes

Cooking time: 8 to 10 hours

Succulent ribs simmered in barbecue sauce taste great with crisp coleslaw and a basket of warm cornbread squares or corn muffins.

 4 **pounds lean beef short ribs, cut into 3- to 4-inch lengths and trimmed of surface fat**
 1 **medium-size onion, finely chopped**
 1 **dry bay leaf**
 1 **medium-size green bell pepper, seeded and chopped**
 3 **cloves garlic, minced or pressed**
 1 **teaspoon dry oregano**
 1½ **teaspoons ground cumin**
 3 **tablespoons chili powder**
 1 **can (about 8 oz.) tomato sauce**
 ¼ **cup catsup**
 1 **tablespoon firmly packed brown sugar**
 3 **tablespoons cider vinegar**
 1½ **teaspoons liquid smoke**
   Salt

Arrange short ribs, bone side down, in a single layer in a shallow baking pan. Bake in a 450° oven until well browned (25 to 30 minutes). Meanwhile, in a 4-quart or larger electric slow cooker, combine onion, bay leaf, bell pepper, garlic, oregano, cumin, and chili powder. In a small bowl, mix tomato sauce, catsup, sugar, vinegar, and liquid smoke; set aside.

Lift ribs from baking pan and place on top of onion mixture in cooker; discard fat in pan. Pour tomato sauce mixture over ribs. Cover and cook at low setting until meat is so tender it pulls away from bones when prodded with a fork (8 to 10 hours).

Lift ribs to a warm serving dish and keep warm. Skim and discard fat from sauce. Season sauce to taste with salt; spoon over ribs. Makes 4 to 6 servings.

Per serving: 358 calories (47% from fat), 32 g protein, 16 g carbohydrates, 19 g total fat (8 g saturated), 91 mg cholesterol, 522 mg sodium

Beef Short Ribs with Chipotle Chiles

Preparation time: About 30 minutes

Cooking time: 8 to 10 hours

This recipe is simplicity itself: just put beef short ribs and a few seasonings in your slow cooker, then let hours of simmering turn the meat meltingly tender. The spirited flavor comes from smoky-tasting chipotle chiles (you can use either the dried or canned variety). Serve the ribs and their sauce with plenty of fluffy rice.

- 4   **pounds lean beef short ribs, cut into 3- to 4-inch lengths and trimmed of surface fat**
- 1   **large onion, finely chopped**
- 2   **dried or canned chipotle chiles**
- ½   **cup beef broth**
-     **Salt**
-     **Cilantro sprigs (optional)**

Arrange short ribs, bone side down, in a single layer in a shallow baking pan. Bake in a 450° oven until well browned (25 to 30 minutes). Meanwhile, in a 4-quart or larger electric slow cooker, combine onion and chiles.

Lift ribs from baking pan and place on top of onion mixture in cooker; discard fat in pan. Pour broth over ribs. Cover and cook at low setting until meat is so tender it pulls away from bones when prodded with a fork (8 to 10 hours).

Lift ribs to a warm serving dish and keep warm. Skim and discard fat from cooking liquid. Use a spoon to break up chiles, then mix them with onions; season mixture to taste with salt and spoon over ribs. Garnish with cilantro sprigs, if desired. Makes 4 to 6 servings.

Per serving: 352 calories (51% from fat), 31 g protein, 12 g carbohydrates, 20 g total fat (8 g saturated), 91 mg cholesterol, 493 mg sodium

Beef Shanks with Root Vegetables

Preparation time: About 25 minutes

Cooking time: 9¼ to 10¼ hours

Strips of turnip and rutabaga combine with carrots, potatoes, and meaty beef shanks in this satisfying cold-weather dish. Long, slow cooking intensifies the naturally sweet flavors of the vegetables.

- 6   **medium-size carrots, cut into halves crosswise, then cut lengthwise into quarters**
- 2   **medium-size onions, cut into eighths**
- 2   **medium-size turnips, peeled and cut into ½-inch-wide, ½-inch-thick sticks**
- 1   **medium-size rutabaga (8 to 10 oz.), peeled and cut into ½-inch-wide, ½-inch-thick sticks**
- 3   **medium-size thin-skinned potatoes (about 1½ lbs. *total*), scrubbed and cut lengthwise into sixths**
- 1   **dry bay leaf**
- ½   **teaspoon *each* coarsely ground pepper and dry thyme**
- 4   **meaty slices beef shank, *each* 1 inch thick (2¼ to 2½ lbs. *total*)**
- 2   **to 3 tablespoons all-purpose flour**
- 1   **cup beef broth**
- 2   **tablespoons cornstarch blended with 2 tablespoons cold water**
-     **Salt**
-     **Chopped parsley**

In a 5-quart or larger electric slow cooker, combine carrots, onions, turnips, rutabaga, potatoes, bay leaf, pepper, and thyme. Coat beef shanks with flour; place on top of vegetables in a single layer. Pour in broth. Cover and cook at low setting until beef is so tender it pulls away from bones when prodded with a fork (9 to 10 hours).

Carefully lift beef and vegetables to a warm deep platter and keep warm. Skim and discard fat from cooking liquid, then blend in cornstarch mixture. Increase cooker heat setting to high; cover and cook, stirring 2 or 3 times, until sauce is thickened (10 to 12 minutes). Season to taste with salt. Spoon a little of the sauce over beef and vegetables; sprinkle with parsley. Serve remaining sauce in a bowl or pitcher to add to taste. Makes 4 servings.

Per serving: 516 calories (27% from fat), 43 g protein, 51 g carbohydrates, 15 g total fat (5 g saturated), 75 mg cholesterol, 406 mg sodium

A welcome beefy fragrance fills the air when you come home to a slow cooker bubbling with Snowy-day Beef Stew (recipe on facing page). Stir in the peas a few minutes before you're ready for dinner.

Snowy-day Beef Stew

Preparation time: About 30 minutes
Cooking time: 8¼ to 10¼ hours

Filled with colorful vegetables, mushrooms, and potatoes, this stew is such a complete dish that you need very few accompaniments—perhaps just a mixed green salad and hot biscuits or crunchy French rolls.

- 1 **medium-size onion, finely chopped**
- 2 **medium-size carrots, cut into ¼-inch-thick slanting slices**
- 1 **pound small thin-skinned potatoes, scrubbed and cut lengthwise into quarters**
- 8 **ounces mushrooms, sliced**
- 2 **to 2¼ pounds lean boneless beef round, trimmed of fat and cut into 1-inch cubes**
- ¼ **cup all-purpose flour**
- 2 **teaspoons dry thyme**
- 1 **can (about 14½ oz.) stewed tomatoes**
- ¼ **cup dry red wine or beef broth**
- 1 **package (about 10 oz.) frozen peas, thawed**
  Salt

In a 3½-quart or larger electric slow cooker, combine onion, carrots, potatoes, and mushrooms. Coat beef cubes with flour, then add to cooker and sprinkle with thyme. Add tomatoes and wine. Cover and cook at low setting until beef is very tender when pierced (8 to 10 hours).

Skim and discard fat from stew, if necessary. Stir in peas. Increase cooker heat setting to high; cover and cook until peas are heated through (10 to 15 more minutes). Season to taste with salt. Makes 6 to 8 servings.

Per serving: 313 calories (15% from fat), 37 g protein, 29 g carbohydrates, 5 g total fat (2 g saturated), 79 mg cholesterol, 276 mg sodium

Sweet-spiced Pot Roast with Chiles

Preparation time: About 15 minutes
Cooking time: 8¼ to 10¼ hours

Familiar braised rump roast gains out-of-the-ordinary flavor when you add chiles, currants, and sweet spices to the cooking pot. Serve the beef and its singular sauce with rice or mashed potatoes.

- 2 **teaspoons olive oil**
- 1 **boneless beef rump roast (3 to 3½ lbs.), trimmed of fat**
- ½ **cup dried currants**
- 6 **cloves garlic, minced or pressed**
- 1 **large can (about 7 oz.) diced green chiles**
- 1 **small dried hot red chile, crushed**
- 1 **teaspoon ground cinnamon**
- ½ **teaspoon *each* dry oregano and dry marjoram**
- ¼ **teaspoon ground allspice**
- ¾ **cup beef broth**
- ¼ **cup red wine vinegar**
- 2 **tablespoons cornstarch blended with 2 tablespoons cold water**
  Salt

Heat oil in a wide nonstick frying pan over medium-high heat; add beef and brown well on all sides. Meanwhile, in a 3-quart or larger electric slow cooker, combine currants, garlic, green chiles, and red chile. Place beef on top of currant mixture; sprinkle with cinnamon, oregano, marjoram, and allspice. Pour in broth and vinegar. Cover and cook at low setting until beef is very tender when pierced (8 to 10 hours).

Lift beef to a warm platter and keep warm. Skim and discard fat from cooking liquid, if necessary; then blend in cornstarch mixture. Increase cooker heat setting to high; cover and cook, stirring 2 or 3 times, until sauce is thickened (10 to 15 more minutes). Season to taste with salt.

To serve, slice beef across the grain. Spoon some of the sauce over beef; serve remaining sauce in a bowl or pitcher to add to taste. Makes 8 to 10 servings.

Per serving: 237 calories (21% from fat), 35 g protein, 10 g carbohydrates, 5 g total fat (1 g saturated), 97 mg cholesterol, 306 mg sodium

Swiss Pot Roast

Preparation time: About 20 minutes
Cooking time: 8¼ to 10¼ hours

Wide noodles are nice with chunky slices of this roast and its marsala-flavored sauce.

  1 boneless beef round tip roast (about 3 lbs.), trimmed of fat
     Ground white pepper
  1 tablespoon butter or margarine
  1 medium-size red onion, thinly sliced
  12 to 16 small carrots (about 10 oz. *total*)
  2 cloves garlic, minced or pressed
  2 ounces sliced prosciutto, cut into strips
  1 teaspoon dry rosemary
  ¾ cup *each* beef broth and dry marsala
  2 tablespoons cornstarch blended with ¼ cup cold water
     Chopped parsley

Sprinkle beef on all sides with white pepper. Melt butter in a wide nonstick frying pan over medium-high heat; add beef and brown well on all sides. Meanwhile, in a 3-quart or larger electric slow cooker, combine onion, carrots, garlic, prosciutto, and rosemary. Place beef on top of onion mixture. Pour in broth and marsala. Cover and cook at low setting until beef is very tender when pierced (8 to 10 hours).

Lift beef and carrots to a warm platter and keep warm. Skim and discard fat from cooking liquid, if necessary; then blend in cornstarch mixture. Increase cooker heat setting to high; cover and cook, stirring 2 or 3 times, until sauce is thickened (10 to 15 more minutes).

To serve, slice beef across the grain. Spoon some of the sauce over meat and carrots; sprinkle with parsley. Serve remaining sauce in a bowl or pitcher to add to taste. Makes 8 servings.

Per serving: 274 calories (29% from fat), 38 g protein, 9 g carbohydrates, 8 g total fat (3 g saturated), 109 mg cholesterol, 363 mg sodium

Cranberry Beef Stew

Preparation time: About 25 minutes
Cooking time: 8½ to 9½ hours

Fresh or frozen cranberries (you can use them without thawing first) lend a ruddy color and tart flavor to this saucy main dish. Serve it with rice or steamed red potatoes.

  ⅓ cup thinly sliced shallots
  1 clove garlic, minced or pressed
  8 ounces small mushrooms, cut into quarters
  2 cups fresh or frozen (unthawed) cranberries
  1 dry bay leaf
  2¾ to 3 pounds lean boneless beef round tip or rump, trimmed of fat and cut into 1-inch cubes
  ⅓ cup all-purpose flour
  1 tablespoon firmly packed brown sugar
  ½ teaspoon pepper
  1 teaspoon dry thyme
  ¾ cup dry red wine
  ⅓ cup beef broth
  ¼ cup Madeira or cream sherry
  2 tablespoons tomato paste
  2 tablespoons cornstarch blended with 2 tablespoons cold water
     Salt
     Chopped parsley

In a 3-quart or larger electric slow cooker, combine shallots, garlic, mushrooms, cranberries, and bay leaf. Coat beef cubes with flour, then add to cooker and sprinkle with sugar, pepper, and thyme. In a small bowl, mix wine, broth, Madeira, and tomato paste; pour over beef mixture. Cover and cook at low setting until beef is very tender when pierced (8 to 9 hours).

Blend cornstarch mixture into stew. Increase cooker heat setting to high; cover and cook, stirring 2 or 3 times, until sauce is thickened (about 20 more minutes). Season to taste with salt; sprinkle with parsley. Makes 8 to 10 servings.

Per serving: 242 calories (22% from fat), 32 g protein, 14 g carbohydrates, 6 g total fat (2 g saturated), 87 mg cholesterol, 153 mg sodium

Beef Round Braised with Tomato & Herbs

Preparation time: About 20 minutes
Cooking time: 8 to 10 hours

Serve thick slices of this moist, tender roast and its herb-seasoned tomato sauce with pasta tubes or twists, such as penne or rotelle.

1 **boneless beef bottom round roast (about 3 lbs.), trimmed of fat**
  Freshly ground pepper
1 **tablespoon olive oil**
1 **medium-size onion, thinly sliced**
1 **medium-size carrot, shredded**
2 **cloves garlic, minced or pressed**
2 **teaspoons Italian herb seasoning; or ½ teaspoon *each* dry basil, marjoram, oregano, and thyme**
1 **large can (about 15 oz.) tomato sauce**
1 **tablespoon Worcestershire**
¼ **cup dry red wine**
  Chopped parsley

Sprinkle beef on all sides with pepper. Heat oil in a wide nonstick frying pan over medium-high heat; add beef and brown well on all sides. Meanwhile, in a 3-quart or larger electric slow cooker, combine onion, carrot, garlic, and herb seasoning. In a small bowl, mix tomato sauce, Worcestershire, and wine; set aside.

Place beef on top of onion mixture; pour tomato sauce mixture over beef. Cover and cook at low setting until beef is very tender when pierced (8 to 10 hours).

Lift beef to a warm platter and keep warm. Skim and discard fat from sauce, if necessary. To serve, slice beef across the grain. Spoon some of the sauce over meat; sprinkle with parsley. Serve remaining sauce in a bowl or pitcher to add to taste. Makes 8 servings.

Per serving: 289 calories (36% from fat), 38 g protein, 7 g carbohydrates, 11 g total fat (3 g saturated), 100 mg cholesterol, 451 mg sodium

Oxtail & Vegetable Stew

Preparation time: About 30 minutes
Cooking time: 10¾ to 12¼ hours

Because the oxtails are oven-browned before they go into the slow cooker, this hearty stew's gravy has a wonderful warm, rich color.

4 **pounds disjointed oxtails, trimmed of fat**
8 **small red thin-skinned potatoes (*each* about 1½ inches in diameter), scrubbed**
2 **medium-size onions, cut lengthwise into sixths**
4 **small turnips (*each* about 2 inches in diameter), peeled and cut into quarters**
8 **small carrots (about 5 oz. *total*)**
4 **cloves garlic, minced or pressed**
½ **teaspoon dry thyme**
1 **dry bay leaf**
¼ **cup all-purpose flour**
1½ **cups beef broth**
2 **tablespoons tomato paste**
1 **cup frozen tiny peas, thawed**
  Salt and pepper

Arrange oxtails in a single layer in a shallow baking pan. Bake in a 450° oven until well browned (25 to 30 minutes). Meanwhile, in a 5-quart or larger electric slow cooker, combine potatoes, onions, turnips, carrots, garlic, thyme, and bay leaf. In a small bowl, mix flour and about ½ cup of the broth until smooth; then stir in remaining broth and tomato paste.

Lift browned oxtails from baking pan and arrange on top of vegetables in cooker; discard fat in pan. Pour broth mixture over oxtails. Cover and cook at low setting until meat is so tender it pulls away from bones when prodded with a fork (10½ to 12 hours).

Lift oxtails to a warm wide serving bowl and keep warm. Skim and discard fat from cooking liquid. Gently mix in peas. Increase cooker heat setting to high; cover and cook until peas are heated through (10 to 12 more minutes). Season to taste with salt and pepper. Spoon vegetable mixture over oxtails. Makes 4 servings.

Per serving: 467 calories (28% from fat), 35 g protein, 49 g carbohydrates, 15 g total fat (0.1 g saturated), 0 mg cholesterol, 673 mg sodium

Cider-simmered Eye of Round

Preparation time: About 15 minutes

Cooking time: 9¾ to 10¼ hours

Slow-cooking is ideal for this lean, compact beef roast; apple cider and sweet spices permeate the meat, creating a complex flavor that's reminiscent of German *Sauerbraten*.

- 2 teaspoons salad oil
- 1 beef eye of round roast (3½ to 4 lbs.), trimmed of fat
- 2 medium-size onions, cut into eighths
- 1 stalk celery, thinly sliced
- 2 cloves garlic, minced or pressed
- 1 teaspoon ground allspice
- ½ teaspoon ground ginger
- ¼ teaspoon pepper
- 1 cup apple cider or apple juice
- 2 tablespoons light molasses
- 2 tablespoons cornstarch blended with 2 tablespoons cold water
  Salt
  Chopped parsley

Heat oil in a wide nonstick frying pan over medium-high heat; add beef and brown well on all sides. Meanwhile, in a 4-quart or larger electric slow cooker, combine onions, celery, and garlic; sprinkle with allspice, ginger, and pepper. In a small bowl, mix cider and molasses. Place beef on top of onion mixture; pour in cider mixture. Cover and cook at low setting until beef is very tender when pierced (9½ to 10 hours).

Lift roast to a warm platter and keep warm. Skim and discard fat from cooking liquid, if necessary; then blend in cornstarch mixture. Increase heat to high; cover and cook, stirring 2 or 3 times, until sauce is thickened (about 15 more minutes). Season to taste with salt.

To serve, remove and discard string from beef, then slice beef across the grain. Spoon some of the sauce over meat; sprinkle with parsley. Serve remaining sauce in a bowl or pitcher to add to taste. Makes 10 to 12 servings.

Per serving: 241 calories (28% from fat), 34 g protein, 8 g carbohydrates, 7 g total fat (2 g saturated), 84 mg cholesterol, 87 mg sodium

Spicy Beef Tongue & Potatoes

Preparation time: About 20 minutes

Cooking time: 10¼ to 12¼ hours

Here's a treat for meat-and-potato fanciers who also dote on the distinctive flavor and texture of fresh—not corned or smoked—beef tongue.

- 2 large onions, finely chopped
- 1 canned chipotle or jalapeño chile
- ¼ cup lightly packed cilantro leaves
- 1 fresh beef tongue (2¾ to 3 lbs.)
- 12 to 16 small red thin-skinned potatoes (*each about 2 inches in diameter*), scrubbed
- 1 can (about 14½ oz.) chicken or beef broth
- 3 tablespoons cornstarch blended with 3 tablespoons cold water
  Salt

In a 4-quart or larger electric slow cooker, combine onions, chile, and cilantro. Place beef tongue on top of onion mixture. Surround with potatoes, then pour in broth. Cover and cook at low setting until tongue is very tender when pierced (10 to 12 hours).

Lift out tongue, place on a carving board, and let stand until cool enough to handle. Pull off and discard tough skin; trim and discard any chunks of fat and bone from back of tongue. Place tongue on a heatproof plate, cover, and keep warm in a 200° oven.

Remove and discard chile from cooking liquid. Lift potatoes to a warm platter and keep warm. Skim and discard fat from cooking liquid, then blend in cornstarch mixture. Increase cooker heat setting to high; cover and cook, stirring 2 or 3 times, until sauce is thickened (12 to 15 more minutes). Season to taste with salt.

To serve, slice tongue; arrange on platter with potatoes. Spoon some of the sauce over tongue and potatoes; serve remaining sauce in a bowl or pitcher to add to taste. Makes 6 to 8 servings.

Per serving: 533 calories (50% from fat), 31 g protein, 34 g carbohydrates, 29 g total fat (12 g saturated), 160 mg cholesterol, 520 mg sodium

*Cider-simmered Eye of Round (recipe on facing page) and its
oniony brown gravy are delicious served with tender egg noodles. Complete
the menu with sparkling cider, a platter of sliced cucumbers and
tomatoes, and a crusty loaf.*

SAUCY SANDWICHES

A slow cooker simplifies the job of making crowd-size batches of saucy hot sandwich fillings. What's more, you can use the cooker's low temperature setting to keep these savory meat mixtures at serving temperature for up to an hour.

Our juicy and flavorful sandwiches take several forms. Try barbecued pork on onion buns or dill-seasoned corned beef on kaiser rolls; or wrap shredded tequila-spiked beef chuck and your choice of savory condiments in warm flour tortillas. And for zesty hero sandwiches, spoon tomato-sauced Italian-style meatballs into long, rectangular sandwich rolls.

Barbecued Pork Sandwiches

Preparation time: About 25 minutes
Cooking time: 9½ to 10½ hours

- 1 **medium-size onion, finely chopped**
- 2 **cloves garlic, minced or pressed**
- 1 **small can (about 4 oz.) diced green chiles**
- 1 **pork shoulder or butt roast (4½ to 5 lbs.), trimmed of fat**
- 1 **teaspoon liquid smoke**
- ⅓ **cup cider vinegar**
- ⅓ **cup apple cider or apple juice**
- ½ **cup prepared barbecue sauce**
- ¼ **cup tomato-based chili sauce**
  Salt and pepper
- 15 **to 20 onion hamburger rolls, split and warmed**

In a 4-quart or larger electric slow cooker, combine onion, garlic, and chiles. Place pork on top; drizzle with liquid smoke. Pour in vinegar, cider, barbecue sauce, and chili sauce. Cover and cook at low setting until pork is so tender it falls into shreds when prodded with a fork (9 to 10 hours).

Carefully lift pork from cooker; skim and discard fat from cooking liquid. Using 2 forks, separate pork into shreds; discard bones and fat. Return shredded pork to cooker; season to taste with salt and pepper. Increase cooker heat setting to high; cover and cook until pork is heated through (25 to 30 more minutes). If desired, reduce heat setting to low to keep pork mixture at serving temperature. Spoon into rolls to serve. Makes 15 to 20 servings.

Per serving: 244 calories (12% from fat), 27 g protein, 25 g carbohydrates, 3 g total fat (0.5 g saturated), 75 mg cholesterol, 440 mg sodium

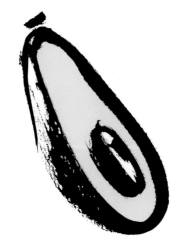

Shredded Beef Burritos

Preparation time: About 25 minutes
Cooking time: 9½ to 10½ hours

- 1 **lean boneless beef chuck roast (2¾ to 3 lbs.), trimmed of fat**
- 4 **teaspoons chili powder**
- 1 **tablespoon olive oil**
- 1 **large onion, finely chopped**
- 2 **cloves garlic, minced or pressed**
- 1 **small can (about 4 oz.) diced green chiles**
- 1 **teaspoon *each* ground cumin and dry oregano**
- 1 **can (about 8 oz.) tomato sauce**
- ¼ **cup tequila (optional)**
  Salt
- 15 **to 18 flour tortillas (*each* 7 to 8 inches in diameter)**
- 2 **medium-size avocados**
- 1 **tablespoon lime juice**
  Condiments (optional): Prepared chile salsa, shredded lettuce, and shredded sharp Cheddar or jack cheese

Sprinkle beef on all sides with 1 teaspoon of the chili powder. Heat oil in a wide nonstick frying pan over medium-high heat. Add beef; brown well on both sides. Meanwhile, in a 4-quart or larger electric slow cooker, combine onion, garlic, and chiles. Place beef on top of onion mixture; then sprinkle with cumin, oregano, and remaining 1 tablespoon chili powder. Pour in tomato sauce and tequila (if used). Cover and cook at low setting until beef is so tender it falls into shreds when prodded with a fork (9 to 10 hours).

Carefully lift beef from cooker; skim and discard fat from cooking liquid. Using 2 forks, separate beef into shreds; discard fat and connective tissue. Return beef to cooker; season to taste with salt. Increase cooker heat setting to high; cover and cook until beef is heated through (15 to 20 more minutes).

Meanwhile, stack tortillas and wrap in foil; heat in a 350° oven until heated through (10 to 15 minutes). Pit, peel, and slice avocados; mix gently with lime juice.

To make each burrito, spoon shredded beef and avocado slices into a warm tortilla; add condiments to taste, if desired. Fold in one end of tortilla; gently roll up tortilla to enclose filling. Makes 15 to 18 burritos.

Per burrito: 261 calories (25% from fat), 21 g protein, 28 g carbohydrates, 7 g total fat (1 g saturated), 45 mg cholesterol, 391 mg sodium

Dilled Corned Beef Buns

Preparation time: About 30 minutes
Cooking time: 8¼ to 10¼ hours

1 **corned beef brisket (3 to 4 lbs.)**
1 **small onion, sliced**
2 **tablespoons dill seeds**
1 **cinnamon stick (about 2 inches long)**
1 **dry bay leaf**
1 **small dried hot red chile**
1 **tablespoon Dijon mustard**
12 **to 15 poppy seed kaiser rolls, split and warmed**
  Condiments (optional): Sliced dill pickles, shredded cabbage, mustard, sliced Swiss cheese

To remove excess salt from corned beef brisket, rinse brisket and place it in a deep 5½- to 6-quart pan; add water to cover. Bring to a boil over high heat,

then reduce heat and simmer for 5 minutes; drain. Repeat this step once more.

Meanwhile, in a 4-quart or larger electric slow cooker, combine onion, dill seeds, cinnamon stick, bay leaf, and chile. Place drained brisket on top of onion mixture; pour in 4 cups water. Cover and cook at low setting until brisket is very tender when pierced (8 to 10 hours).

Lift brisket from cooker and let cool slightly. Meanwhile, pour liquid in cooker through a strainer placed

over a bowl. Discard solids in strainer; then measure ⅔ cup of the cooking liquid and return it to cooker. Blend in mustard.

Cut brisket into thin bite-size slices, removing and discarding fat. Return sliced meat to cooker; mix lightly with mustard mixture. Increase cooker heat setting to high; cover and cook until meat is heated through (15 to 20 more minutes). If desired, reduce heat setting to low to keep mixture at serving temperature. Spoon into warmed rolls to serve. If desired, add condiments to each sandwich to taste. Makes 12 to 15 servings.

Per serving: 363 calories (43% from fat), 20 g protein, 31 g carbohydrates, 17 g total fat (5 g saturated), 80 mg cholesterol, 1,253 mg sodium

Snappy Meatball Heroes

Pictured on page 3

Preparation time: About 20 minutes
Cooking time: 5½ to 6 hours

1 **egg**
½ **teaspoon salt**
½ **teaspoon Italian herb seasoning; or ⅛ teaspoon *each* dry basil, marjoram, oregano, and thyme**
¼ **teaspoon crushed red pepper flakes**
2 **cloves garlic, minced or pressed**
¼ **cup finely chopped onion**
1 **pound extra-lean ground beef**
8 **ounces ground veal or ground turkey**
½ **cup fine dry bread crumbs**
⅓ **cup grated Parmesan cheese**
1 **large can (about 15 oz.) tomato sauce**
¼ **cup dry red wine**
6 **to 8 rectangular sandwich rolls, split and warmed**
  Condiments (optional): Roasted red and yellow pepper strips, thinly sliced red onion, sliced ripe olives, sliced provolone or mozzarella cheese

In a large bowl, beat egg with salt, herb seasoning, red pepper flakes, and garlic. Add chopped onion, beef, veal, crumbs, and Parmesan cheese; mix well. Shape mixture into 1½-inch balls. Place meatballs in a 5-quart or larger electric slow cooker.

In same bowl, mix tomato sauce and wine; pour over meatballs. Cover and cook at low setting until meatballs are no longer pink in center; cut to test (5½ to 6 hours).

Carefully lift meatballs from cooker and place 3 or 4 in each split roll; moisten with a little of the sauce from cooker. If desired, add condiments to each sandwich to taste. Makes 6 to 8 servings.

Per serving: 437 calories (39% from fat), 28 g protein, 39 g carbohydrates, 19 g total fat (6 g saturated), 108 mg cholesterol, 947 mg sodium

Seasoned with lemon and herbs, savory Mediterranean-style Lamb Stew
(recipe on facing page) simmers all day; the zucchini slices are added just
before serving, the better to keep their crisp texture and bright color. To add
still more color to each plate, serve steamed carrots alongside the stew.

30

Mediterranean-style Lamb Stew

Preparation time: About 20 minutes

Cooking time: 7¾ to 8¾ hours

Complement the Near Eastern flavor of this juicy lamb and zucchini stew with spoonfuls of hot cooked brown rice or fragrant rice pilaf.

- 1 **medium-size onion, finely chopped**
- 2 **cloves garlic, minced or pressed**
- 2 **strips lemon peel (colored part only),** *each* **about ½ by 2 inches**
- 2 **pounds lean boneless lamb (such as shoulder, leg, or loin), trimmed of fat and cut into 1-inch cubes**
- 3 **tablespoons all-purpose flour**
- ¼ **teaspoon pepper**
- ½ **teaspoon dry marjoram**
- 1 **tablespoon sugar**
- 1 **can (about 14½ oz.) diced tomatoes**
- ⅓ **cup dry white wine or chicken broth**
- 2 **tablespoons cornstarch blended with 2 tablespoons cold water**
- 6 **small zucchini (about 12 oz.** *total***), cut into ½-inch-thick slices**
  Salt
  Finely shredded lemon peel (optional)

In a 3-quart or larger electric slow cooker, combine onion, garlic, and lemon peel strips. Coat lamb cubes with flour; add to cooker and sprinkle with pepper, marjoram, and sugar. Pour in tomatoes and wine. Cover and cook at low setting until lamb is very tender when pierced (7½ to 8½ hours).

Skim and discard fat from stew, if necessary; remove and discard lemon peel strips. Blend in cornstarch mixture. Stir in zucchini and increase cooker heat setting to high; cover and cook until zucchini is just tender to bite (15 to 20 more minutes). Season to taste with salt; garnish with shredded lemon peel, if desired. Makes 6 servings.

Per serving: 279 calories (34% from fat), 31 g protein, 14 g carbohydrates, 11 g total fat (4 g saturated), 100 mg cholesterol, 221 mg sodium

Savory Lamb Stew

Preparation time: About 30 minutes

Cooking time: 8 to 8½ hours

Juniper berries, peppercorns, and cloves—spices usually preferred for cooking wild game such as venison—season this aromatic lamb stew. Try it with wild rice or red potatoes.

- 1 **large onion, finely chopped**
- 3 **cloves garlic, minced or pressed**
- 8 **ounces small mushrooms, cut into quarters**
  Peel of 1 orange (colored part only), cut from orange in a spiral
- 10 *each* **whole black peppercorns and juniper berries, crushed**
- 1 **dry bay leaf**
- 2½ **to 3 pounds lean boneless lamb (such as leg, loin, or shoulder), trimmed of fat and cut into 1-inch cubes**
- ⅓ **cup all-purpose flour**
- 1 **tablespoon powdered sugar**
- 1 **teaspoon dry thyme**
- ½ **teaspoon** *each* **salt and ground nutmeg**
- ¼ **teaspoon ground cloves**
- 1 **cup dry red wine or beef broth**
- ¼ **cup brandy**
- 2 **tablespoons cornstarch blended with 2 tablespoons cold water**
  Chopped chives

In a 3-quart or larger electric slow cooker, combine onion, garlic, mushrooms, orange peel, peppercorns, juniper berries, and bay leaf. Coat lamb cubes with flour; add to cooker and sprinkle with sugar, thyme, salt, nutmeg, and cloves. Pour in wine and brandy. Cover; cook at low setting until lamb is very tender when pierced (7½ to 8 hours).

Skim and discard fat from stew, if necessary. Remove and discard orange peel and bay leaf; blend in cornstarch mixture. Increase cooker heat setting to high; cover and cook, stirring 2 or 3 times, until sauce is thickened (about 20 more minutes). Sprinkle with chives. Makes 8 servings.

Per serving: 252 calories (27% from fat), 34 g protein, 11 g carbohydrates, 7 g total fat (3 g saturated), 100 mg cholesterol, 237 mg sodium

Umatilla County Lamb Stew with Spring Vegetables

Preparation time: About 25 minutes
Cooking time: 7¾ to 8¾ hours

Members of a northeastern Oregon cooking club devised this homey dish to celebrate their region's abundance. Serve the tempting medley of lamb, barley, and vegetables with new potatoes.

> 1   **large onion, finely chopped**
> 3   **medium-size carrots, sliced**
> 1   **medium-size turnip, peeled and chopped**
> ⅓   **cup pearl barley, rinsed and drained**
> 2½   **to 3 pounds lean boneless lamb (such as shoulder, leg, or loin), trimmed of fat and cut into 1-inch cubes**
> ¼   **cup all-purpose flour**
> ½   **teaspoon *each* pepper and dry marjoram**
> 1   **can (about 14½ oz.) beef broth**
> 8   **ounces green beans, cut into 1-inch lengths**
> 1½   **cups shelled fresh peas; or 1½ cups frozen tiny peas, thawed**
>   **Salt**

In a 3-quart or larger electric slow cooker, combine onion, carrots, turnip, and barley. Coat lamb cubes with flour, then add to cooker and sprinkle with pepper and marjoram. Pour in broth. Cover and cook at low setting until lamb is very tender when pierced (7½ to 8½ hours).

When lamb is almost done, cook beans. Bring about 4 cups water to a boil in a 2½- to 3-quart pan; add beans and cook, uncovered, until just tender to bite (4 to 7 minutes). Drain well.

Skim and discard fat from stew, if necessary. Stir in beans and peas. Increase cooker heat setting to high; cover and cook until peas are tender to bite (8 to 10 minutes). Season to taste with salt. Makes 8 servings.

Per serving: 328 calories (31% from fat), 35 g protein, 21 g carbohydrates, 11 g total fat (4 g saturated), 103 mg cholesterol, 318 mg sodium

Lamb Shanks with Apricot Couscous

Preparation time: About 25 minutes
Cooking time: 7¾ to 9¼ hours

Fragrant apricot wine echoes the sweet-tart tang of dried apricots in a fluffy couscous to serve with spicy braised lamb shanks. To bring all the flavors together, steam the couscous in the liquid that remains in the cooker after the meat is done.

> 4   **lamb shanks (3½ to 4 lbs. *total*), bones cracked**
> 1   **large onion, finely chopped**
> 1   **cinnamon stick (about 2 inches long)**
> 1½   **teaspoons ground coriander**
> 1   **teaspoon ground ginger**
> ½   **teaspoon ground cumin**
> ¼   **teaspoon ground allspice**
> 1¼   **cups chicken broth**
> ¼   **cup apricot or orange muscat dessert wine**
> ¾   **cup coarsely chopped dried apricots**
> 1½   **cups couscous**
>   **Mint sprigs (optional)**

Place lamb shanks in a single layer in a shallow baking pan. Bake in a 450° oven until well browned (20 to 25 minutes). Meanwhile, in a 4-quart or larger electric slow cooker, combine onion, cinnamon stick, coriander, ginger, cumin, and allspice. Lift lamb from baking pan and place on top of onion mixture; discard fat in pan. Pour broth over lamb. Cover and cook at low setting until lamb is so tender it pulls away from bones when prodded with a fork (7½ to 9 hours).

Lift lamb to a warm deep platter and keep warm. Skim and discard fat from cooking liquid; then measure liquid. You need 2¼ cups; if necessary, pour off some of the liquid or add enough hot water to make 2¼ cups. Return liquid to cooker and increase heat setting to high. Stir in wine and apricots, then couscous. Cover and let stand until liquid has been absorbed (about 10 more minutes). Spoon couscous around lamb; garnish with mint sprigs, if desired. Makes 4 servings.

Per serving: 610 calories (18% from fat), 48 g protein, 75 g carbohydrates, 12 g total fat (5 g saturated), 126 mg cholesterol, 468 mg sodium

Red-cooked Lamb Shanks

Preparation time: About 25 minutes

Cooking time: 7¼ to 8¼ hours

"Red cooking" is a traditional Chinese braising technique that's tailor-made for an electric slow cooker. Here, oven-browned lamb shanks bubble gently in a mixture of ginger, sherry, and soy sauce (the soy gives the meat a brownish-red tinge, hence the term "red cooking").

- 4 **lamb shanks (3½ to 4 lbs.** *total*)**, bones cracked**
- 3 **tablespoons grated fresh ginger**
- 3 **green onions, thinly sliced**
- 2 **cloves garlic, minced or pressed**
- ¼ **cup water**
- ½ **cup dry sherry**
- ⅓ **cup soy sauce**
- 2 **tablespoons sugar**
- 1½ **tablespoons cornstarch blended with 2 table-spoons cold water**
  Slivered green onions
- 4 **cups hot cooked pasta or rice**

Place lamb shanks in a single layer in a shallow baking pan. Bake in a 450° oven until well browned (20 to 25 minutes). Meanwhile, spread ginger, sliced onions, and garlic in bottom of a 4-quart or larger electric slow cooker. Lift lamb from baking pan and place on top of ginger mixture. Discard fat in pan, then pour in water and stir to dissolve browned bits; pour mixture over lamb. In a small bowl, mix sherry, soy sauce, and sugar; pour over lamb. Cover and cook at low setting until lamb is so tender it pulls away from bones when prodded with a fork (7 to 8 hours).

Lift lamb to a warm deep platter and keep warm. Skim and discard fat from cooking liquid, then blend in cornstarch mixture. Increase cooker heat setting to high; cover and cook, stirring 2 or 3 times, until sauce is slightly thickened (about 10 more minutes). Pour sauce over lamb; sprinkle with slivered onions. Serve lamb and sauce with pasta. Makes 4 servings.

Per serving: 514 calories (19% from fat), 47 g protein, 56 g carbohydrates, 11 g total fat (4 g saturated), 125 mg cholesterol, 1,512 mg sodium

Braised Lamb & Vegetables with Mint

Preparation time: About 20 minutes

Cooking time: 7¼ to 8¼ hours

Colorful vegetables (you add the quick-cooking zucchini and peas just before serving) prettily set off lamb chops braised in a cinnamon-scented sauce. You might accompany the dish with a bulgur wheat pilaf.

- 1 **medium-size onion, finely chopped**
- 2 **cloves garlic, minced or pressed**
- 2 **medium-size carrots, cut into ¼-inch-thick slanting slices**
- 1 **teaspoon ground cinnamon**
- ⅓ **cup chopped fresh mint or 1½ teaspoons dry mint**
- 4 **lamb shoulder blade or arm chops, cut about 1 inch thick (2¼ to 2½ lbs.** *total*)**, edges trimmed of fat**
  Freshly ground pepper
- 2 **tablespoons all-purpose flour**
- ½ **cup beef or chicken broth**
- 2 **medium-size zucchini (about 8 oz.** *total*)**, cut into ⅛-inch-thick slanting slices**
- 1 **cup frozen peas, thawed**
  Salt

In a 4-quart or larger electric slow cooker, combine onion, garlic, and carrots; sprinkle with cinnamon and mint. Sprinkle lamb chops with pepper, dust with flour, and arrange over onion mixture, overlapping slightly. Pour in broth. Cover and cook at low setting until lamb is very tender when pierced (7 to 8 hours).

Lift lamb to a warm platter and keep warm. Skim and discard fat from cooking liquid, then add zucchini and peas. Increase cooker heat setting to high; cover and cook until zucchini is just tender to bite (12 to 15 more minutes). Season to taste with salt. Spoon vegetables and liquid over and around chops. Makes 4 to 6 servings.

Per serving: 226 calories (26% from fat), 28 g protein, 14 g carbohydrates, 6 g total fat (2 g saturated), 82 mg cholesterol, 219 mg sodium

Lamb Shoulder Cassoulet

Preparation time: About 1¼ hours (including standing time)

Cooking time: 9 to 10½ hours

Flavorful lamb shoulder is featured in this sturdy bean stew, an easy-to-assemble version of a traditional dish from the southwest of France.

- 1   pound dried Great Northern beans
- 2   quarts water
- ½   cup diced baked ham
- 1   large onion, thinly sliced
- 1   large carrot, shredded
- 5   cloves garlic, thinly sliced
- 1   dry bay leaf
- 1   teaspoon *each* dry thyme and paprika
- ½   teaspoon dry rosemary
- ¼   teaspoon baking soda
- 12   to 14 ounces skinless, boneless chicken thighs
- 2   pounds lean boneless lamb shoulder, trimmed of fat and cut into 1-inch cubes
- ¼   cup all-purpose flour
- 1   can (about 14½ oz.) chicken broth
- 1   medium-size tomato, peeled, seeded, and chopped
- 2   tablespoons tomato paste
- 12   ounces kielbasa, cut into ½-inch-thick slices
     Crispy Bread Crumbs (recipe follows)
- ¼   cup chopped parsley

Rinse and sort through beans. In a deep 3½- to 4-quart pan, bring water to a boil over high heat. Add beans. Let water return to a boil; then boil, uncovered, for 2 minutes. Remove pan from heat, cover, and let stand for 1 hour. Drain and rinse beans, discarding cooking water.

In a 4-quart or larger electric slow cooker, combine ham, onion, carrot, garlic, bay leaf, thyme, paprika, rosemary, and baking soda. Add beans. Rinse chicken and pat dry. Coat chicken and lamb cubes with flour; distribute over beans, then pour in broth. Cover and cook at low setting until beans are very tender to bite (8½ to 10 hours).

Stir in tomato, tomato paste, and kielbasa. Increase cooker heat setting to high; cover and cook until sausage is hot (25 to 30 more minutes). Prepare Crispy Bread Crumbs. Sprinkle cassoulet with parsley; spoon on crumbs. Makes 10 to 12 servings.

Crispy Bread Crumbs. Heat 1 tablespoon **olive oil** in a wide nonstick frying pan over medium heat. Stir in 1½ cups **soft bread crumbs** and 1 clove **garlic,** minced or pressed. Cook, stirring often, until crumbs are crisp and brown (about 5 minutes).

Per serving: 467 calories (35% from fat), 39 g protein, 36 g carbohydrates, 18 g total fat (6 g saturated), 107 mg cholesterol, 764 mg sodium

Italian Pork Stew

Preparation time: About 30 minutes

Cooking time: 8 to 10 hours

Serve golden polenta and a green salad to complement this simple, aromatic stew's hearty tomato sauce.

- 1   large onion, finely chopped
- 3   cloves garlic, minced or pressed
- ½   cup chopped baked ham
- 8   ounces mushrooms, cut into quarters
- 2   to 2½ pounds boneless pork shoulder or butt, trimmed of fat and cut into 1-inch cubes
- 3   tablespoons all-purpose flour
- 2   teaspoons Italian herb seasoning; or ½ teaspoon *each* dry basil, marjoram, oregano, and thyme
- 1   can (2 oz.) anchovy fillets, drained, chopped
- 1   can (about 14½ oz.) crushed tomatoes
- 2   tablespoons *each* tomato paste and dry red wine
     Chopped parsley

In a 3-quart or larger electric slow cooker, combine onion, garlic, ham, and mushrooms. Coat pork cubes with flour, then add to cooker and sprinkle with herb seasoning and anchovies. Pour in tomatoes. In a small bowl, mix tomato paste and wine; add to cooker. Cover and cook at low setting until pork is very tender when pierced (8 to 10 hours). Skim and discard fat from stew, if necessary. Sprinkle with parsley. Makes 6 to 8 servings.

Per serving: 306 calories (40% from fat), 35 g protein, 11 g carbohydrates, 13 g total fat (4 g saturated), 107 mg cholesterol, 651 mg sodium

Lamb Shoulder Cassoulet (recipe on facing page), thick with smoky sausage, chicken, and tender lamb chunks, looks and tastes very much like the traditional French dish. But our slow-cooker version is far simpler to prepare.

Lamb Shoulder Chops with Lima Beans

Preparation time: About 15 minutes

Cooking time: 6¼ to 7¼ hours

Three members of the onion family and a whisper of saffron perfume these moist shoulder chops.

8 shallots (about 4 oz. *total*)

8 cloves garlic

2 leeks (white and pale green parts only), thinly sliced

4 lamb shoulder blade or arm chops, cut about 1 inch thick (2¼ to 2½ lbs. *total*), edges trimmed of fat

   Freshly ground pepper

2 tablespoons all-purpose flour

¼ teaspoon saffron threads, crushed; or ⅛ teaspoon ground saffron

½ cup dry white wine

1 package (about 10 oz.) frozen baby lima beans, thawed

   Salt

Peel shallots and separate into cloves, if necessary. Peel garlic cloves and crush coarsely with the side of a knife. In a 4-quart or larger electric slow cooker, combine shallots, garlic, and leeks. Sprinkle lamb chops with pepper, dust with flour, and arrange over shallot mixture, overlapping slightly. Sprinkle with saffron; pour in wine. Cover and cook at low setting until lamb is very tender when pierced (6 to 7 hours).

Spoon beans around lamb. Increase cooker heat setting to high; cover and cook until beans are tender to bite (15 to 20 more minutes). Lift lamb to a warm platter and keep warm. Skim and discard fat from shallot mixture in cooker. Spoon beans and shallot mixture around chops; season to taste with salt. Makes 4 to 6 servings.

Per serving: 383 calories (31% from fat), 38 g protein, 28 g carbohydrates, 13 g total fat (4 g saturated), 110 mg cholesterol, 157 mg sodium

Green Chile & Pork Carnitas

Preparation time: About 15 minutes

Cooking time: 8 to 10 hours

Baking time: 30 to 35 minutes

You simmer this pork roast for 8 hours or more—then brown it in a hot oven, shred it, spice it with salsa, and spoon it into steamy-warm tortillas.

2 large carrots, chopped

2 large onions, chopped

1 pork shoulder or butt roast (5 to 5½ lbs.), trimmed of fat

1 teaspoon *each* ground cumin, ground coriander, dry oregano, and chili powder

3 cups water

1 jar (about 12 oz.) green chile salsa

1 large can (about 7 oz.) diced green chiles

½ cup thinly sliced green onions

2 to 4 dozen warm corn or flour tortillas (*each* 6 to 8 inches in diameter)

In a 4-quart or larger electric slow cooker, combine carrots and chopped onions; place pork on top, then sprinkle with cumin, coriander, oregano, and chili powder. Pour in water. Cover and cook at low setting until pork is so tender it falls into shreds when prodded with a fork (8 to 10 hours). Discard cooking liquid and vegetables (or reserve to use in soup).

Carefully lift pork from cooker and place in a 9-by 13-inch baking pan. Bake in a 400° oven until well browned (20 to 25 minutes). Spoon off and discard fat. Using 2 forks, separate pork into shreds; discard bones and fat. Stir in salsa, chiles, and green onions; return pan to oven until mixture is heated through (about 10 minutes).

Return pork mixture to slow cooker and keep warm at low setting; or serve in a warm bowl. To eat, spoon pork mixture into tortillas. Makes 12 to 15 servings (2 to 3 filled tortillas *each*).

Per serving: 458 calories (35% from fat), 37 g protein, 37 g carbohydrates, 18 g total fat (4 g saturated), 109 mg cholesterol, 732 mg sodium

Spiced Pork Stew

Preparation time: About 20 minutes

Cooking time: 7½ to 8½ hours

If you like sweet-sour flavors, you'll enjoy these pork chunks simmered with red wine, raisins, and cinnamon. Try the dish with baked sweet potatoes and warm cornbread or corn muffins.

- 2 medium-size onions, cut into eighths
- ¼ cup raisins
- 2 cloves garlic, minced or pressed
- 1 dry bay leaf
- 1 cinnamon stick (about 2 inches long)
- 2 pounds boneless fresh leg of pork, trimmed of fat and cut into 1-inch cubes
- 3 tablespoons all-purpose flour
- 2 teaspoons ground cumin
- 2 tablespoons firmly packed brown sugar
- 1 cup dry red wine or chicken broth
- 1 can (about 6 oz.) tomato paste
- ¼ cup red wine vinegar
   Salt

In a 3-quart or larger electric slow cooker, combine onions, raisins, garlic, bay leaf, and cinnamon stick. Coat pork cubes with flour, then add to cooker and sprinkle with cumin and sugar. In a small bowl, mix wine, tomato paste, and vinegar; pour over pork. Cover and cook at low setting until pork is very tender when pierced (7½ to 8½ hours).

Skim and discard fat from stew, if necessary. Season to taste with salt. Makes 6 servings.

Per serving: 299 calories (26% from fat), 33 g protein, 22 g carbohydrates, 9 g total fat (3 g saturated fat), 103 mg cholesterol, 313 mg sodium

Creole Pork Roast

Preparation time: About 15 minutes

Cooking time: 7¾ to 8¼ hours

There's plenty of sauce to go with this colorful braised roast. Serve the sliced meat and spicy gravy over rice—preferably the fragrant, Louisiana-grown "popcorn" variety.

- 1 pork loin roast (4 to 4½ lbs.), trimmed of fat (reserve trimmings)
- 1 medium-size onion, thinly sliced
- 3 cloves garlic, minced or pressed
- 1 medium-size green bell pepper, seeded and chopped
- 1 dry bay leaf
- ½ teaspoon *each* black pepper and dry thyme
- ¼ teaspoon ground red pepper (cayenne)
- 1 can (about 14½ oz.) crushed tomatoes
- 2 tablespoons cornstarch blended with 2 tablespoons cold water
   Salt
   Chopped parsley

Heat pork fat trimmings in a wide nonstick frying pan over medium-high heat; add pork roast and brown well on all sides. Meanwhile, in a 4-quart or larger electric slow cooker, combine onion, garlic, bell pepper, and bay leaf. Place pork on top of onion mixture; sprinkle with black pepper, thyme, and red pepper. Pour in tomatoes. Cover and cook at low setting until pork is very tender when pierced (7½ to 8 hours).

Carefully lift pork to a warm platter and keep warm. Skim and discard fat from cooking liquid, then blend in cornstarch mixture. Increase cooker heat setting to high; cover and cook, stirring 2 or 3 times, until sauce is thickened (10 to 15 more minutes). Season to taste with salt.

To serve, slice pork across the grain. Spoon some of the sauce over pork; sprinkle with parsley. Serve remaining sauce in a bowl or pitcher to add to taste. Makes 10 to 12 servings.

Per serving: 198 calories (32% from fat), 39 g protein, 5 g carbohydrates, 9 g total fat (3 g saturated), 107 mg cholesterol, 184 mg sodium

Crisp, golden Cornmeal-Yogurt Biscuits are an irresistible
complement to Creamy Pork & Apples (recipe on facing page). To soak up
every drop of the luscious sauce, spoon it over a split biscuit.

Creamy Pork & Apples with Cornmeal Biscuits

Preparation time: About 30 minutes

Cooking time: 7¾ to 8¾ hours

Baking time: 10 to 12 minutes

Golden biscuits are a homey topping—and a hearty accompaniment—for this luscious stew. Complete the meal with white wine and steamed green beans.

- 1 **small onion, finely chopped**
- 3 **cloves garlic, minced or pressed**
- 2 **large tart green apples, peeled, cored, and sliced**
- 2 **teaspoons** *each* **sugar and dry sage**
- ¼ **teaspoon** *each* **ground white pepper and ground nutmeg**
- 2 **to 2½ pounds boneless fresh leg of pork or pork loin, trimmed of fat and cut into 1-inch cubes**
- 3 **tablespoons all-purpose flour**
- ½ **cup dry white wine**
  Cornmeal-Yogurt Biscuits (recipe follows)
- 1½ **tablespoons cornstarch**
- ⅓ **cup whipping cream**
  Salt

In a 3-quart or larger electric slow cooker, combine onion, garlic, and apples; sprinkle with sugar, sage, white pepper, and nutmeg. Coat pork cubes with flour, then arrange over apple mixture. Pour in wine. Cover and cook at low setting until pork is very tender when pierced (7½ to 8½ hours).

When pork is almost done, prepare Cornmeal-Yogurt Biscuits. While biscuits are baking, mix cornstarch and cream in a small bowl; blend into pork mixture. Increase cooker heat setting to high; cover and cook until sauce is hot and bubbly (10 to 15 more minutes). Season to taste with salt. Arrange 6 to 8 of the biscuits around edge of pork mixture in cooker; serve remaining biscuits in a basket. Makes 6 to 8 servings.

Cornmeal-Yogurt Biscuits. In a large bowl, stir together 1½ cups **all-purpose flour,** ½ cup **yellow cornmeal,** 1 tablespoon **baking powder,** 1 teaspoon **sugar,** and ½ teaspoon **salt.** Dice ⅓ cup cold **butter** or margarine; with a pastry blender or 2 knives, cut butter into flour mixture until mixture resembles coarse crumbs. Add ¾ cup **plain nonfat yogurt;** stir just until mixture forms a sticky dough. Gather dough into a ball and knead gently on a floured board; then roll or pat out about ½ inch thick. Using a floured 2½-inch cutter, cut dough into 12 rounds. Place about 1 inch apart on an ungreased baking sheet. Bake in a 450° oven until golden brown (10 to 12 minutes). Serve hot.

Per serving: 511 calories (37% from fat), 36 g protein, 44 g carbohydrates, 21 g total fat (10 g saturated), 136 mg cholesterol, 532 mg sodium

Apricot-Pineapple Country-style Ribs

Preparation time: About 30 minutes

Cooking time: 7½ to 9 hours

A sweet, ginger-seasoned sauce forms as these simple-to-prepare ribs simmer. Serve with hot rice and a spinach salad.

- 3½ **to 4 pounds country-style pork spareribs, trimmed of surface fat**
- ¼ **cup soy sauce**
- ½ **cup apricot-pineapple jam**
- 2 **tablespoons grated fresh ginger**

Arrange spareribs in a single layer in a shallow baking pan. Bake in a 450° oven until well browned (25 to 30 minutes). Meanwhile, in a small bowl, mix soy sauce, jam, and ginger.

Lift spareribs from baking pan and arrange in a 4-quart or larger electric slow cooker; discard fat in pan. Pour soy sauce mixture over spareribs. Cover and cook at low setting until spareribs are very tender when pierced (7½ to 9 hours).

Lift spareribs to a warm platter and keep warm. Skim and discard fat from sauce; spoon sauce over spareribs. Makes 6 servings.

Per serving: 471 calories (65% from fat), 21 g protein, 20 g carbohydrates, 34 g total fat (12 g saturated), 97 mg cholesterol, 756 mg sodium

Pork Loin with Winter Fruits

Preparation time: About 15 minutes

Cooking time: 7½ to 8½ hours

Dried apricots, prunes, and apples go into the cooker with boneless pork roast, turning plump and juicy as the meat simmers. Accompany with asparagus or broccoli spears and baked potatoes.

- 1 boneless pork loin roast (2¾ to 3 lbs.), trimmed of fat
  Freshly grated nutmeg
- 2 teaspoons salad oil
- 1 large onion, finely chopped
- ½ cup *each* pitted prunes and dried apricots
- 1 cup dried apple slices
- 1 teaspoon dry mustard
- ½ teaspoon ground cinnamon
- ¼ teaspoon salt
- ½ cup dry sherry
- 2 tablespoons lemon juice
- 1 tablespoon honey

Sprinkle pork on all sides with nutmeg. Heat oil in a wide nonstick frying pan over medium-high heat; add pork and brown well on all sides. Meanwhile, in a 4-quart or larger electric slow cooker, combine onion, prunes, apricots, and apples; sprinkle with mustard, cinnamon, and salt. In a small bowl, mix sherry, lemon juice, and honey.

Place pork on top of fruit mixture; pour sherry mixture over pork. Cover and cook at low setting until pork is very tender when pierced (7½ to 8½ hours).

Lift pork to a warm platter. To serve, slice pork across the grain; spoon fruits around meat. Makes 8 servings.

Per serving: 355 calories (33% from fat), 35 g protein, 24 g carbohydrates, 13 g total fat (4 g saturated), 98 mg cholesterol, 186 mg sodium

Wine-simmered Pork Chops with Walnuts

Preparation time: About 15 minutes

Cooking time: 7½ to 8½ hours

Succulent pork chops cook slowly in a simple sauce of onions, garlic, and red wine. Before serving, sprinkle the meat with toasted walnuts for a crunchy accent.

- 1 medium-size onion, thinly sliced
- 2 cloves garlic, minced or pressed
- ¼ cup finely chopped parsley
- 4 center-cut loin pork chops (1¾ to 2 lbs. *total*), edges trimmed of fat
  Freshly ground pepper
- 2 tablespoons all-purpose flour
- ⅓ cup dry red wine or beef broth
- ½ cup coarsely chopped walnuts
  Salt

In a 4-quart or larger electric slow cooker, combine onion, garlic, and 3 tablespoons of the parsley. Sprinkle pork chops with pepper, dust with flour, and arrange over onion mixture, overlapping slightly if necessary. Pour in wine. Cover and cook at low setting until pork is very tender when pierced (7½ to 8½ hours).

Shortly before pork is done, spread walnuts in a shallow baking pan and bake in a 350° oven until toasted (8 to 10 minutes). Set aside.

Lift pork chops to a warm platter and keep warm. Skim and discard fat from onion mixture, if necessary; then season to taste with salt. Spoon onion mixture over chops; sprinkle with walnuts and remaining 1 tablespoon parsley. Makes 4 servings.

Per serving: 350 calories (51% from fat), 34 g protein, 9 g carbohydrates, 20 g total fat (4 g saturated), 90 mg cholesterol, 99 mg sodium

Baby Back Ribs & Sauerkraut

Preparation time: About 30 minutes

Cooking time: 8 to 10 hours

These meaty little ribs, generously seasoned with paprika, cook along with a mixture of sauerkraut and fresh red cabbage in a crimson tomato sauce.

- 3 **pounds pork baby back ribs, trimmed of surface fat**
- ¼ **teaspoon pepper**
- 3 **tablespoons sweet Hungarian paprika**
- 1 **large can (about 27 oz.) sauerkraut, drained, rinsed, and drained again**
- 4 **cups shredded red cabbage**
- 4 **cloves garlic, minced or pressed**
- 1 **can (about 8 oz.) tomato sauce**
- 2 **tablespoons cornstarch**
- ¼ **cup dry white wine**
  Salt
  Chopped parsley

Sprinkle ribs on all sides with pepper and 1 tablespoon of the paprika; arrange in a single layer in a shallow baking pan. Bake in a 450° oven until well browned (25 to 30 minutes). Meanwhile, in a 4-quart or larger electric slow cooker, combine sauerkraut, cabbage, and garlic. Sprinkle with remaining 2 tablespoons paprika. In a small bowl, mix tomato sauce, cornstarch, and wine; pour over sauerkraut mixture.

Lift ribs from baking pan and cut into serving-size pieces; discard fat in pan. Arrange ribs on top of sauerkraut mixture. Cover and cook at low setting until ribs are very tender when pierced (8 to 10 hours).

Lift ribs to a warm plate and keep warm. Skim and discard fat from sauerkraut mixture, if necessary; season to taste with salt. Spoon sauerkraut mixture into a warm serving dish and top with ribs. Sprinkle with parsley. Makes 4 to 6 servings.

Per serving: 495 calories (64% from fat), 29 g protein, 16 g carbohydrates, 35 g total fat (13 g saturated), 117 mg cholesterol, 713 mg sodium

Braised Pork with Vinegar

Preparation time: About 30 minutes

Cooking time: 8 to 10 hours

If you've only tasted jicama crunchy and raw, you'll be happily surprised by the sweet, water chestnut–like flavor of the steamed vegetable. Here, strips of jicama harmonize nicely with Asian seasonings in a savory sauce for country-style spareribs.

- 3 **pounds country-style pork spareribs, trimmed of surface fat**
- 8 **to 12 medium-size carrots**
- 1 **pound jicama, peeled and cut lengthwise into ½-inch-wide, ½-inch-thick sticks**
- 6 **to 8 cloves garlic, peeled and crushed**
- 6 **thin slices fresh ginger**
- 1 **cup seasoned rice vinegar; or 1 cup white wine vinegar plus ¼ cup sugar**
- ¼ **cup soy sauce**
  Cilantro or parsley sprigs

Arrange spareribs in a single layer in a shallow baking pan. Bake in a 450° oven until well browned (25 to 30 minutes). Meanwhile, in a 4-quart or larger electric slow cooker, combine carrots, jicama, garlic, and ginger. Lift spareribs from baking pan and arrange on top of carrot mixture; discard fat in pan. Pour vinegar and soy sauce over spareribs. Cover and cook at low setting until spareribs are very tender when pierced (8 to 10 hours).

Carefully lift spareribs and vegetables to a warm deep platter and keep warm. Skim and discard fat from cooking liquid; drizzle a little of the liquid over spareribs and vegetables. Garnish with cilantro sprigs. Serve remaining liquid in a pitcher to pour over ribs to taste. Makes 4 servings.

Per serving: 636 calories (58% from fat), 29 g protein, 39 g carbohydrates, 41 g total fat (15 g saturated), 117 mg cholesterol, 1,156 mg sodium

Dilled Swedish Veal Roast

Preparation time: About 20 minutes

Cooking time: 7¾ to 9¼ hours

Tender veal roast in a creamy dill sauce is delicious sliced and served with steamed small red potatoes.

   1 tablespoon butter or margarine
   1 boned, rolled, tied veal shoulder or leg roast (2¾ to 3 lbs.)
   8 ounces mushrooms, cut into quarters
  24 to 36 very small carrots or 6 to 8 medium-size carrots
   2 tablespoons chopped fresh dill or 2 teaspoons dry dill weed
  ⅛ teaspoon ground white pepper
  ¼ cup lemon juice
  ½ cup dry white wine
   3 tablespoons cornstarch
  ⅓ cup whipping cream
     Salt
     Twist of lemon peel and dill sprigs (optional)

Melt butter in a wide nonstick frying pan over medium-high heat. Add veal and brown well on all sides, then place in a 4-quart or larger electric slow cooker. Surround veal with mushrooms and carrots (if using medium-size carrots, first cut each in half crosswise; then cut lengthwise into quarters). Sprinkle with chopped dill and white pepper. Pour in lemon juice and wine. Cover and cook at low setting until veal is very tender when pierced (7½ to 9 hours).

Carefully lift veal to a warm deep platter. Using a slotted spoon, lift carrots and mushrooms from cooker and arrange around veal; keep warm. In a small bowl, mix cornstarch and cream; blend into liquid in cooker. Increase cooker heat setting to high; cover and cook, stirring 2 or 3 times, until sauce is thickened (15 to 20 more minutes). Season to taste with salt.

To serve, remove and discard strings from veal; slice veal across the grain. Spoon some of the sauce over veal and vegetables; if desired, garnish with lemon peel and dill sprigs. Serve remaining sauce in a bowl or pitcher to add to taste. Makes 6 to 8 servings.

Per serving: 312 calories (32% from fat), 39 g protein, 13 g carbohydrates, 11 g total fat (5 g saturated), 178 mg cholesterol, 222 mg sodium

Lemon-Herb Veal Stew

Preparation time: About 20 minutes

Cooking time: 7¾ to 8¼ hours

Lemon peel and juice contribute to the vibrant flavor of this juicy veal dish. Serve it with tiny pasta and steamed, nutmeg-dusted baby carrots.

   1 leek (white and pale green parts only), thinly sliced
   3 cloves garlic, minced or pressed
   1 tablespoon dry tarragon
  ½ teaspoon *each* grated lemon peel, dry thyme, and ground white pepper
  ¼ teaspoon dry sage
  2½ to 3 pounds boneless veal shoulder or leg, trimmed of fat and cut into 1-inch cubes
  ⅓ cup all-purpose flour
  ¾ cup dry white wine
  ¼ cup lemon juice
   1 tablespoon cornstarch
  ¼ cup whipping cream
     Salt
     Tarragon or sage sprigs; or chopped parsley
     Thin lemon slices

In a 3-quart or larger electric slow cooker, combine leek, garlic, dry tarragon, lemon peel, thyme, white pepper, and sage. Coat veal cubes with flour, then add to cooker and pour in wine and lemon juice. Cover and cook at low setting until veal is very tender when pierced (7½ to 8 hours).

In a small bowl, mix cornstarch and cream; blend into stew. Increase cooker heat setting to high; cover and cook, stirring 2 or 3 times, until sauce is thickened (about 15 more minutes). Season to taste with salt. Garnish with tarragon sprigs and lemon slices. Makes 8 servings.

Per serving: 233 calories (28% from fat), 32 g protein, 8 g carbohydrates, 7 g total fat (3 g saturated), 143 mg cholesterol, 152 mg sodium

*Dilled Swedish Veal Roast (recipe on facing page) is robust
fare, delicately flavored. Accompany the moist slices with little red
potatoes and a loaf of sturdy rye bread.*

Osso Buco with Risotto

Preparation time: About 30 minutes
Cooking time: 8 ½ to 10 ½ hours

Meaty veal shanks, their bones filled with succulent marrow, simmer to tenderness in your slow cooker. Once the veal is done, lift it out; then cook the risotto in the flavorful juices left in the cooker.

- 4 to 6 pounds veal shanks, cut crosswise into 3-inch sections
- 1 small onion, finely chopped
- 3 cloves garlic, minced or pressed
- 2 tablespoons grated lemon peel
- ½ cup finely chopped parsley
- 1 teaspoon dry thyme
- 1 can (about 14½ oz.) chicken broth
- 1½ cups dry white wine
- ¼ teaspoon saffron threads, crushed; or ⅛ teaspoon ground saffron (optional)
- 1½ cups arborio or short-grain rice
- ⅓ cup grated Parmesan cheese

Arrange veal shanks in a single layer in a shallow baking pan. Bake in a 450° oven until well browned (25 to 30 minutes). Meanwhile, in a 5-quart or larger electric slow cooker, combine onion, 2 cloves of the garlic, 1 tablespoon of the lemon peel, ¼ cup of the parsley, and thyme.

Lift veal from baking pan and arrange on top of onion mixture; discard fat in pan. Pour broth and wine over veal. Cover and cook at low setting until veal is so tender it pulls away from bones when prodded with a fork (8 to 10 hours). Carefully lift veal to a warm wide, deep platter and keep warm.

If using saffron, stir into liquid in cooker. Stir in rice. Increase cooker heat setting to high; cover and cook until almost all liquid is absorbed and rice is tender to bite (25 to 30 minutes). Meanwhile, in a small bowl, mix remaining 1 clove garlic, 1 tablespoon lemon peel, and ¼ cup parsley; set aside.

To serve, lightly mix cheese into risotto. Spoon risotto around veal; sprinkle with parsley mixture. Makes 4 to 6 servings.

Per serving: 437 calories (15% from fat), 39 g protein, 51 g carbohydrates, 7 g total fat (3 g saturated), 121 mg cholesterol, 558 mg sodium

Spicy Rice Meatballs

Preparation time: About 20 minutes
Cooking time: 5 ½ to 6 hours

This slow-cooker variation on a long-time family favorite is especially easy to assemble. Chili powder and mild green chiles update the flavor.

- 1 egg
- ½ teaspoon salt
- ½ teaspoon Italian herb seasoning; or ⅛ teaspoon *each* dry basil, marjoram, oregano, and thyme
- ¼ teaspoon pepper
- 1 clove garlic, minced or pressed
- ¼ cup finely chopped onion
- 1 pound extra-lean ground beef
- 8 ounces ground veal or ground turkey
- ½ cup *each* long-grain white rice and fine dry bread crumbs
- 1 large can (about 15 oz.) tomato sauce
- ½ cup tomato juice
- 1 teaspoon chili powder
- 1 small can (about 4 oz.) diced green chiles

In a large bowl, beat egg with salt, herb seasoning, and pepper. Add garlic, onion, beef, veal, rice, and crumbs; mix well. Shape mixture into 1½-inch balls. Place meatballs in a 5-quart or larger electric slow cooker.

In same bowl, mix tomato sauce, tomato juice, chili powder, and chiles; pour over meatballs. Cover and cook at low setting until meatballs are no longer pink in center and rice is tender; cut a meatball to test (5½ to 6 hours). Gently lift meatballs to a warm serving dish and keep warm. Skim and discard fat from sauce, if necessary. Stir sauce, then spoon over meatballs. Makes 6 servings.

Per serving: 368 calories (42% from fat), 26 g protein, 27 g carbohydrates, 17 g total fat (7 g saturated), 119 mg cholesterol, 959 mg sodium

Red Beans, Sausage & Rice

Preparation time: About 1 ¼ hours (including standing time)

Cooking time: 8 ½ to 10 hours

Here's a zesty interpretation of a well-known New Orleans entrée. To serve, spoon the meaty blend of beans, sausage slices, and ham over fluffy rice.

- 1 **pound dried small red beans**
- 2 **quarts plus 3 cups water**
- 1 **smoked ham hock (about 1 lb.)**
- 1 **large onion, finely chopped**
- 1 **green bell pepper, seeded and chopped**
- 2 **dry bay leaves**
- 1 **pound andouille or linguisa sausages, cut into ¼-inch-thick slices**
- 1 **teaspoon ground red pepper (cayenne)**
- ½ **teaspoon dry thyme**
- ¼ **teaspoon baking soda**
- 2 **to 4 tablespoons cider vinegar**
- 8 **to 10 cups hot cooked rice**
  Sliced green onions

Rinse and sort through beans. In a deep 3½- to 4-quart pan, bring 2 quarts of the water to a boil over high heat. Add beans. Let water return to a boil; then boil, uncovered, for 2 minutes. Remove pan from heat, cover, and let stand for 1 hour. Drain and rinse beans, discarding cooking water.

While beans are standing, in a 4-quart or larger electric slow cooker, combine ham hock, chopped onion, bell pepper, bay leaves, and sausage slices. Sprinkle with red pepper, thyme, and baking soda. Stir beans into sausage mixture; pour in remaining 3 cups water. Cover and cook at low setting until beans are very tender to bite (8½ to 10 hours).

Lift out ham hock and let stand until cool enough to handle. Skim and discard fat from bean mixture. Remove and discard fat and bone from ham; tear meat into bite-size pieces and return to bean mixture. Stir in vinegar.

To serve, spoon rice onto plates or into shallow bowls, then ladle on bean mixture and sprinkle with green onions. Makes 8 to 10 servings.

Per serving: 605 calories (21% from fat), 27 g protein, 92 g carbohydrates, 14 g total fat (5 g saturated), 41 mg cholesterol, 802 mg sodium

Smoked Sausage & Lentils

Preparation time: About 20 minutes

Cooking time: 8 to 8 ½ hours

Fresh zucchini, stirred in shortly before serving, adds a colorful finishing touch to this spicy combination.

- 1 **pound lentils, rinsed and drained**
- 1 **small onion, finely chopped**
- 1 **stalk celery, finely chopped**
- ¼ **teaspoon *each* ground cloves and baking soda**
- 4 **medium-size pear-shaped (Roma-type) tomatoes, seeded and chopped**
- 2 **cans (about 14½ oz. *each*) chicken broth**
- 1 **pound smoked sausage or kielbasa, cut into ¼-inch-thick slanting slices**
- 3 **medium-size zucchini (about 12 oz. *total*), cut into thin slanting slices**
  Salt

In a 3-quart or larger electric slow cooker, combine lentils, onion, celery, cloves, baking soda, and tomatoes; pour in broth. Cover and cook at low setting until lentils are very tender when mashed with a fork (7½ to 8 hours).

Stir in sausage slices and zucchini. Increase cooker heat setting to high; cover and cook until zucchini is just tender-crisp to bite and sausage is heated through (about 30 more minutes). Season to taste with salt. Makes 6 to 8 servings.

Per serving: 471 calories (40% from fat), 29 g protein, 43 g carbohydrates, 21 g total fat (7 g saturated), 46 mg cholesterol, 1,170 mg sodium

Simmer colorful Portuguese Garlic Chicken (recipe on
page 48) all day in your slow cooker, then finish it under the broiler
to brown and crisp the skin.

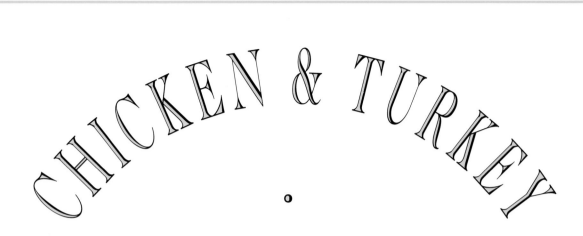

CHICKEN & TURKEY

Poultry simmered in a slow cooker is an invitation to delicious dining—and whether you choose chicken, turkey, or another bird, you can always count on fork-tenderness. Even at a slow cooker's unhurried pace, though, poultry is usually ready to serve sooner than most meats—so choose the recipes in this chapter when you'll be home for dinner within 8 hours (or less) after switching on your cooker.

Pictured on page 46

Portuguese Garlic Chicken

Preparation time: About 15 minutes

Cooking time: 7¾ to 8¼ hours

What gives this sophisticated dish its haunting flavor? Plenty of garlic—but that's only the beginning. Golden raisins, port, mustard, and flecks of ham also blend in the savory, long-simmered sauce.

    1   medium-size onion, thinly sliced
    6   cloves garlic, thinly sliced
    2   medium-size pear-shaped (Roma-type)
        tomatoes, seeded and chopped
    ⅓   cup chopped baked ham
    ½   cup golden raisins
    1   chicken (3¼ to 3¾ lbs.)
    ½   cup port wine
    ¼   cup brandy
    1   tablespoon Dijon mustard
    2   tablespoons tomato paste
    1½ tablespoons cornstarch blended with 2
        tablespoons cold water
    1   tablespoon red wine vinegar
        Salt
        Parsley sprigs and tomato wedges

In a 4-quart or larger electric slow cooker, combine onion, garlic, tomatoes, ham, and raisins. Reserve chicken neck and giblets for other uses; rinse chicken inside and out and pat dry. Tuck wingtips under; tie drumsticks together, if desired. Place chicken on top of onion mixture. Mix port, brandy, mustard, and tomato paste; pour over chicken. Cover; cook at low setting until meat near thighbone is very tender when pierced (7½ to 8 hours).

Carefully lift chicken to rack of a broiler pan. Broil 4 to 6 inches below heat until golden brown (about 5 minutes). Transfer to a warm platter; keep warm. Skim and discard fat from cooking liquid; blend in cornstarch mixture. Increase cooker heat setting to high; cover and cook, stirring 2 or 3 times, until sauce is thickened (about 10 more minutes). Stir in vinegar; season to taste with salt.

To serve, garnish chicken with parsley sprigs and tomato wedges. Carve bird; top with some of the sauce. Serve remaining sauce in a bowl to add to taste. Makes 4 to 6 servings.

Per serving: 446 calories (42% from fat), 42 g protein, 23 g carbohydrates, 20 g total fat (6 g saturated), 129 mg cholesterol, 408 mg sodium

Chicken in Riesling with Grapes

Preparation time: About 20 minutes

Cooking time: 6¾ to 7¼ hours

True to its origins in Alsace—the region of eastern France bordering Germany—this creamy, mushroom-sauced chicken is good with noodles.

    ¼   cup chopped shallots
    1   clove garlic, minced or pressed
    6   ounces mushrooms, sliced
    ¼   teaspoon dry tarragon
    1   chicken (3¼ to 3½ lbs.), cut into quarters
        Ground white pepper
    ½   cup Riesling or other dry white wine
    2   tablespoons cornstarch
    ⅓   cup whipping cream
    ½   cup seedless green grapes
    1   to 2 tablespoons lemon juice
        Salt

In a 4-quart or larger electric slow cooker, combine shallots, garlic, mushrooms, and tarragon. Rinse chicken and pat dry; then arrange, overlapping pieces slightly, on top of mushroom mixture. Sprinkle with white pepper; pour in wine. Cover and cook at low setting until meat near thighbone is very tender when pierced (6½ to 7 hours).

Carefully lift chicken to a warm platter and keep warm. Skim and discard fat from cooking liquid. In a small bowl, mix cornstarch and cream; blend into cooking liquid. Increase cooker heat setting to high; cover and cook, stirring 2 or 3 times, until sauce is thickened (about 10 more minutes). Stir in grapes, then season to taste with lemon juice and salt. Cover and cook for 3 to 5 more minutes. To serve, spoon sauce over chicken. Makes 4 servings.

Per serving: 569 calories (55% from fat), 50 g protein, 12 g carbohydrates, 35 g total fat (12 g saturated), 208 mg cholesterol, 196 mg sodium

Chicken in Red Wine

Preparation time: About 25 minutes

Cooking time: 6¾ to 7¼ hours

Here's a robust slow-cooker rendition of a traditional French *coq au vin*. Serve the saucy dish with rice-shaped pasta, or with the tender strands scooped from a baked or microwaved spaghetti squash.

⅓ cup sliced shallots

5 cloves garlic, sliced

1 medium-size carrot, shredded

8 ounces mushrooms, sliced

1 dry bay leaf

½ teaspoon dry thyme

8 ounces pear-shaped (Roma-type) tomatoes, seeded and chopped

1 chicken (3¼ to 3½ lbs.), cut up

Freshly ground pepper

1 tablespoon tomato paste

2 tablespoons brandy

½ cup dry red wine

3 tablespoons all-purpose flour blended with 2 tablespoons butter or margarine (at room temperature)

Salt

Chopped parsley

In a 4-quart or larger electric slow cooker, combine shallots, garlic, carrot, mushrooms, bay leaf, thyme, and tomatoes. Rinse chicken and pat dry; arrange, overlapping pieces slightly, over tomato mixture. Sprinkle with pepper. Mix tomato paste, brandy, and wine; pour over chicken. Cover and cook at low setting until meat near thighbone is very tender when pierced (6½ to 7 hours).

Carefully lift chicken to a warm serving dish; keep warm. Skim and discard fat from cooking liquid; blend in flour mixture. Increase cooker heat setting to high; cover and cook, stirring 2 or 3 times, until sauce is thickened (12 to 15 more minutes). Season sauce to taste with salt; pour over chicken. Sprinkle with parsley. Makes 4 to 6 servings.

Per serving: 481 calories (60% from fat), 41 g protein, 13 g carbohydrates, 29 g total fat (10 g saturated), 163 mg cholesterol, 233 mg sodium

Garlic Chicken with Tomatoes & Potatoes

Preparation time: About 15 minutes

Cooking time: 6¾ to 7¼ hours

Hearty and boldly flavored, this one-pot chicken dinner needs only a green salad and crusty bread as accompaniments.

4 to 6 small red thin-skinned potatoes (*each about 2 inches in diameter*), scrubbed and cut lengthwise into quarters

12 ounces pear-shaped (Roma-type) tomatoes, cut lengthwise into quarters

12 cloves garlic, peeled and crushed

½ teaspoon herbes de Provence; or ½ teaspoon dry thyme and a pinch of fennel seeds

1 chicken (3¼ to 3½ lbs.), cut up

¼ teaspoon coarsely ground pepper

1 teaspoon dry mustard

½ cup dry white wine

2 tablespoons cornstarch blended with 2 tablespoons cold water

Salt

Chopped parsley

In a 4-quart or larger electric slow cooker, combine potatoes, tomatoes, garlic, and herbes de Provence. Rinse chicken and pat dry; then arrange, overlapping pieces slightly, on top of potato mixture. Sprinkle with pepper. In a small bowl, mix mustard and wine; pour over chicken. Cover and cook at low setting until meat near thighbone is very tender when pierced (6½ to 7 hours).

Carefully lift chicken and potatoes to a warm serving dish; keep warm. Skim and discard fat from cooking liquid, then blend in cornstarch mixture. Increase cooker heat setting to high; cover and cook, stirring 2 or 3 times, until sauce is thickened (about 10 more minutes). Season sauce to taste with salt; pour over chicken and potatoes. Sprinkle with parsley. Makes 4 to 6 servings.

Per serving: 512 calories (50% from fat), 41 g protein, 22 g carbohydrates, 28 g total fat (8 g saturated), 153 mg cholesterol, 161 mg sodium

Caribbean Chicken in Rum

Preparation time: About 15 minutes
Cooking time: 6¾ to 7¼ hours

Tender, rum-sauced chicken quarters, topped with a sprinkling of crunchy almonds, are good with fluffy rice. Sautéed bananas make a suitably tropical accompaniment.

- ½ cup sliced red onion
- 2 tablespoons grated fresh ginger
- 2 cloves garlic, minced or pressed
- 1 small jar (about 2 oz.) sliced pimentos, drained
- 1 chicken (3¼ to 3½ lbs.), cut into quarters
  Freshly ground nutmeg
- 2 tablespoons lime juice
- ¼ teaspoon crushed red pepper flakes
- ⅓ cup dark rum
- 2 tablespoons cornstarch blended with 2 tablespoons cold water
- ¼ cup slivered almonds
  Salt
  Lime slices

In a 4-quart or larger electric slow cooker, combine onion, ginger, garlic, and pimentos. Rinse chicken and pat dry; then arrange, overlapping pieces slightly, on top of onion mixture. Sprinkle with nutmeg. In a small bowl, mix lime juice, red pepper flakes, and rum; pour over chicken. Cover and cook at low setting until meat near thighbone is very tender when pierced (6½ to 7 hours).

Carefully lift chicken to a warm platter and keep warm. Skim and discard fat from cooking liquid, then blend in cornstarch mixture. Increase cooker heat setting to high; cover and cook, stirring 2 or 3 times, until sauce is thickened (about 10 more minutes).

Meanwhile, toast almonds in a small nonstick frying pan over medium heat until golden brown (5 to 8 minutes), stirring occasionally. Set aside.

To serve, season sauce to taste with salt. Spoon sauce over chicken; sprinkle with almonds and garnish with lime slices. Makes 4 servings.

Per serving: 543 calories (55% from fat), 51 g protein, 9 g carbohydrates, 33 g total fat (8 g saturated), 186 mg cholesterol, 190 mg sodium

Chicken with Tomatillos & Rice

Preparation time: About 15 minutes
Cooking time: 6¾ to 7¾ hours

Cilantro and tart tomatillos flavor this simple, spicy chicken (look for the canned tomatillos in Mexican grocery stores or in your supermarket's Mexican food section). Serve the chicken and rice with a green salad and warm tortillas.

- 1 small onion, finely chopped
- 2 cloves garlic, minced or pressed
- 1 small can (about 4 oz.) diced green chiles
- 1 teaspoon ground cumin
- 1 can (about 11 oz.) tomatillos
- 1 chicken (3¼ to 3½ lbs.), cut up
- ½ teaspoon chili powder
- ¼ to ½ cup chicken broth, if necessary
- 1 cup long-grain white rice
- ¼ cup lightly packed cilantro leaves

In a 4-quart or larger electric slow cooker, combine onion, garlic, chiles, and cumin. Drain tomatillos, reserving liquid. Cut tomatillos into halves; add tomatillo halves to onion mixture. Rinse chicken and pat dry; then arrange, overlapping pieces slightly, on top of tomatillos. Sprinkle with chili powder. Measure tomatillo liquid; add broth, if necessary, to make 1½ cups. Pour liquid over chicken. Cover and cook at low setting until meat near thighbone is very tender when pierced (6 to 7 hours).

Carefully lift chicken to a warm serving dish; cover lightly and keep warm in a 200° oven. Skim and discard fat from cooking liquid; stir in rice. Increase cooker heat setting to high; cover and cook, stirring once or twice, until rice is just tender to bite (35 to 40 minutes). Spoon rice around chicken; sprinkle with cilantro. Makes 4 to 6 servings.

Per serving: 567 calories (44% from fat), 43 g protein, 35 g carbohydrates, 27 g total fat (8 g saturated), 152 mg cholesterol, 425 mg sodium

Island flavors mingle in Caribbean Chicken in Rum (recipe on facing page), a saucy quartered bird sparked with ginger, nutmeg, lime, and crushed red chiles. To complement the chicken, offer banana quarters—first dipped in lime juice and cinnamon sugar, then lightly sautéed.

GAME HENS & MORE

Chicken and turkey aren't the only birds that simmer to flavorsome succulence in a slow cooker. Other kinds of poultry, such as Cornish game hens and duck, turn out just as successfully. And slow-cooker rabbit stews are delicious, too.

For best results with our game hen dishes, use a cooker that's broader than it's deep. You might prepare a brown rice pilaf to spoon beside the tarragon- and tomato-seasoned birds; with the second dish, try tender fresh fettuccine or other pasta strands. The third recipe—hen halves glazed with honey and mustard—includes its own accompaniment of quartered small potatoes.

The braised quartered duck, cloaked in a spicy, chile-dotted orange sauce, is excellent with black beans or fluffy rice. With the pungently seasoned rabbit, serve thin-skinned potatoes; or offer tagliarini or another pasta of your choice.

Tarragon & Tomato Game Hens

Preparation time: About 15 minutes
Cooking time: 7¾ to 8¼ hours

- 4 medium-size shallots, thinly sliced
- 2 cloves garlic, minced or pressed
- 2 large tomatoes, peeled, seeded, and chopped
- 4 teaspoons dry tarragon
- 2 Cornish game hens (about 1¼ lbs. *each*), thawed if frozen

Salt and freshly ground pepper
- ¼ cup tarragon vinegar or white wine vinegar
Tarragon sprigs (optional)

In a 4-quart or larger electric slow cooker, combine shallots, garlic, tomatoes, and dry tarragon. With poultry shears or a knife, split hens lengthwise through breastbone and along one side of backbone. Rinse hen halves, pat dry, and sprinkle with salt and pepper; then place halves, cut sides down, on top of tomato mixture. Drizzle with vinegar. Cover and cook at low setting until meat near thighbone is very tender when pierced (7½ to 8 hours).

Carefully lift hens to a warm deep platter; keep warm. Skim and discard fat from cooking liquid; pour liquid into a wide frying pan. Bring to a boil over high heat; then boil, stirring often, until reduced to 1 cup (about 3 minutes). Pour sauce over hens. Garnish with tarragon sprigs, if desired. Makes 4 servings.

Per serving: 330 calories (48% from fat), 35 g protein, 7 g carbohydrates, 17 g total fat (5 g saturated), 110 mg cholesterol, 112 mg sodium

Game Hens with Sun-dried Tomatoes

Preparation time: About 15 minutes
Cooking time: 7¾ to 8¼ hours

- ¼ cup chopped shallots
- ½ teaspoon dry marjoram
- ⅓ cup coarsely chopped sun-dried tomatoes
- 2 Cornish game hens (about 1¼ lbs. *each*), thawed if frozen
Salt and freshly ground pepper
- ½ cup dry white wine
- ⅓ cup whipping cream
Chopped parsley

In a 4-quart or larger electric slow cooker, combine shallots, marjoram, and dried tomatoes. With poultry shears or a knife, split hens lengthwise through breastbone and along one side of backbone. Rinse hen halves, pat dry, and sprinkle with salt and pepper; then place halves, cut sides down, on top of shallot mixture. Drizzle with wine. Cover and cook at low setting until meat near thighbone is very tender when pierced (7½ to 8 hours).

Carefully lift hens to a warm deep platter; keep warm. Skim and discard fat from cooking liquid, if necessary; then pour liquid into a wide frying pan and stir in cream. Bring to a boil over high heat; boil, stirring often, until reduced to about ⅔ cup (about 5 minutes). Pour sauce over hens; sprinkle with parsley. Makes 4 servings.

Per serving: 416 calories (56% from fat), 38 g protein, 7 g carbohydrates, 26 g total fat (9 g saturated), 158 mg cholesterol, 154 mg sodium

Honey-Mustard Game Hens

Preparation time: About 15 minutes
Cooking time: 7¾ to 8¼ hours

8 **small thin-skinned potatoes (*each* 1½ to 2 inches in diameter), cut lengthwise into quarters**
1 **teaspoon dry thyme**
2 **Cornish game hens (about 1¼ lbs. *each*), thawed if frozen**
 Salt and freshly ground pepper
2 **tablespoons *each* honey and Dijon mustard**
¼ **cup dry white wine**
 Chopped parsley

In a 4-quart or larger electric slow cooker, combine potatoes and thyme. With poultry shears or a knife, split hens lengthwise through breastbone and along one side of backbone. Rinse hen halves, pat dry, and sprinkle with salt and pepper; then place halves, cut sides down, on top of potatoes. In a small bowl, mix honey, mustard, and wine; pour over hens. Cover and cook at low setting until meat near thighbone is very tender when pierced (7½ to 8 hours).

Carefully lift hens to a warm deep platter, then spoon potatoes around hens; keep warm. Skim and discard fat from cooking liquid, if necessary; pour liquid into a wide frying pan. Bring to a boil over high heat; then boil, stirring often, until reduced to about ½ cup (about 5 minutes). Pour sauce over hens; sprinkle with parsley. Makes 4 servings.

Per serving: 456 calories (36% from fat), 37 g protein, 35 g carbohydrates, 18 g total fat (5 g saturated), 110 mg cholesterol, 340 mg sodium

Citrus- & Chile-braised Duck

Preparation time: About 40 minutes
Cooking time: 6¼ to 7¼ hours

1 **duck (4½ to 5 lbs.), thawed if frozen**
1 **small can (about 4 oz.) diced green chiles**
1 **clove garlic, minced or pressed**
1 **tablespoon grated orange peel**
⅛ **teaspoon crushed red pepper flakes**
1 **teaspoon ground cumin**
¼ **cup *each* orange juice and lime juice**
1½ **tablespoons cornstarch blended with 2 tablespoons cold water**
 Salt
 Orange and lime slices

Reserve duck neck and giblets for other uses, if desired; then pull off and discard lumps of fat from duck. Rinse duck inside and out; pat dry. With poultry shears or a knife, split duck lengthwise through breastbone and along both sides of backbone. Discard backbone. Cut each duck half in half; with a fork, pierce skin all over. Then place duck quarters, skin sides up, in a baking pan. Bake in a 425° oven until golden brown (about 30 minutes).

Meanwhile, in a 5-quart or larger electric slow cooker, combine chiles, garlic, orange peel, red pepper flakes, and cumin. Place browned duck quarters, skin sides up, on top of chile mixture, overlapping slightly. Discard fat from baking pan. Pour orange juice and lime juice over duck. Cover; cook at low setting until meat near thighbone is very tender when pierced (6 to 7 hours).

Carefully lift duck to a warm serving dish; keep warm. Skim and discard fat from cooking liquid, then blend in cornstarch mixture. Increase cooker heat setting to high; cover and cook, stirring 2 or 3 times, until sauce is thickened (about 10 minutes). Season sauce to taste with salt; pour over duck. Garnish with orange and lime slices. Makes 4 servings.

Per serving: 725 calories (73% from fat), 39 g protein, 8 g carbohydrates, 58 g total fat (20 g saturated), 172 mg cholesterol, 298 mg sodium

Rabbit in Blue Cheese & Mustard Sauce

Preparation time: About 15 minutes
Cooking time: 6¾ to 8¾ hours

1 **frying rabbit (2½ to 3 lbs.), cut up**
 Freshly ground pepper
1½ **teaspoons *each* dry thyme and dry savory**
1 **dry bay leaf**
¼ **cup Dijon mustard**
3 **tablespoons dry white wine**
1 **tablespoon cornstarch**
⅓ **cup whipping cream**
½ **cup crumbled blue-veined cheese**

Rinse rabbit and pat dry; then arrange, overlapping pieces slightly, in a 4-quart or larger electric slow cooker. Sprinkle with pepper, thyme, and savory; insert bay leaf between 2 rabbit pieces. Mix mustard and wine; pour over rabbit. Cover and cook at low setting until meat in thickest part is very tender when pierced (6½ to 8½ hours).

Carefully lift rabbit to a warm serving dish; keep warm. Mix cornstarch and cream; blend into cooking liquid. Increase cooker heat setting to high; cover and cook, stirring 2 or 3 times, until sauce is thickened (about 10 more minutes). Add ¼ cup of the cheese, cover, and let stand for 3 to 5 minutes; stir until cheese is melted. Pour sauce over rabbit; sprinkle with remaining ¼ cup cheese. Makes 4 to 6 servings.

Per serving: 385 calories (49% from fat), 43 g protein, 5 g carbohydrates, 21 g total fat (9 g saturated), 139 mg cholesterol, 603 mg sodium

The golden-and-green combination of egg and spinach fettuccine known as "straw and hay" repeats the colors—and rounds out the flavors—of piquant Tuscan Chicken with Olives & Peppers (recipe on facing page).

Tuscan Chicken with Olives & Peppers

Preparation time: About 15 minutes

Cooking time: 6¾ to 7¼ hours

The tiny Italian-style pickled peppers called *peperoncini* impart their distinctive flavor to this piquant dish. Try it over green and golden fettuccine; serve crisp breadsticks alongside. For dessert, offer fresh fruit and a wedge of cheese.

  8 **to 12 peperoncini, rinsed and drained**
  ½ **cup sliced ripe olives**
  6 **cloves garlic, minced or pressed**
  1 **chicken (3¼ to 3½ lbs.), cut up**
  ½ **teaspoon paprika**
  ⅓ **cup lemon juice**
  1½ **tablespoons cornstarch blended with 2 tablespoons cold water**
     Salt

In a 4-quart or larger electric slow cooker, combine peperoncini, olives, and garlic. Rinse chicken and pat dry; then arrange, overlapping pieces slightly, on top of olive mixture. Sprinkle with paprika. Pour in lemon juice. Cover and cook at low setting until meat near thighbone is very tender when pierced (6½ to 7 hours).

Carefully lift chicken to a warm serving dish and keep warm. Skim and discard fat from cooking liquid, then blend in cornstarch mixture. Increase cooker heat setting to high; cover and cook, stirring 2 or 3 times, until sauce is thickened (about 10 more minutes). Season sauce to taste with salt; spoon over chicken. Makes 4 to 6 servings.

Per serving: 440 calories (58% from fat), 39 g protein, 6 g carbohydrates, 33 g total fat (9 g saturated), 152 mg cholesterol, 649 mg sodium

Chicken & Green Onion Curry

Preparation time: About 25 minutes

Cooking time: 6¾ to 7¼ hours

Like our Ginger-Beef Curry (page 16), this dish starts with a homemade blend of pungent spices; slow cooking brings all the flavors together. Hot steamed rice is the perfect accompaniment.

  1 **medium-size onion, thinly sliced**
  3 **cloves garlic, minced or pressed**
  1 **tablespoon grated fresh ginger**
  1 **cinnamon stick (about 2 inches long)**
  ½ **teaspoon *each* ground cumin and crushed red pepper flakes**
  1 **teaspoon ground turmeric**
  ¼ **teaspoon *each* ground cloves and ground cardamom**
  1 **chicken (3¼ to 3½ lbs.), cut up and skinned**
  ½ **cup chicken broth**
  2 **tablespoons cornstarch blended with 2 tablespoons cold water**
     Salt
  ¼ **cup lightly packed cilantro leaves**
  ½ **cup sliced green onions**

In a 4-quart or larger electric slow cooker, lightly mix thinly sliced onion, garlic, ginger, cinnamon stick, cumin, red pepper flakes, turmeric, cloves, and cardamom. Rinse chicken and pat dry; then arrange, overlapping pieces slightly, on top of onion mixture. Pour in broth. Cover and cook at low setting until meat near thighbone is very tender when pierced (6½ to 7 hours).

Carefully lift chicken to a warm serving dish and keep warm. Skim and discard fat from cooking liquid, if necessary; remove and discard cinnamon stick. Blend in cornstarch mixture. Increase cooker heat setting to high; cover and cook, stirring 2 or 3 times, until sauce is thickened (about 10 more minutes). Season sauce to taste with salt; stir in cilantro and green onions. Pour sauce over chicken. Makes 4 to 6 servings.

Per serving: 207 calories (22% from fat), 32 g protein, 7 g carbohydrates, 5 g total fat (1 g saturated), 103 mg cholesterol, 216 mg sodium

Chicken & Pinto Beans

Preparation time: About 1 hour (including standing time)
Cooking time: 8½ to 9½ hours

When chilly weather calls for cozy, warming suppers, try this dish: chicken pieces nestled in herbed beans flavored with ham, salami, and bell pepper. Serve the juicy soup-stew in wide, shallow bowls, with hot garlic bread on the side.

- 1 cup dried pinto beans
- 2 quarts water
- 1 small onion, finely chopped
- 1 medium-size carrot, shredded
- ½ cup finely chopped green bell pepper
- 2 cloves garlic, minced or pressed
- 2 cups diced baked ham
- 1 dry bay leaf
- 1 teaspoon dry thyme
- ¼ teaspoon baking soda
- 1 chicken (3¼ to 3½ lbs.), cut up and skinned
- 2 tablespoons all-purpose flour
- 1 cup chicken broth

- 1 medium-size pear-shaped (Roma-type) tomato, seeded and chopped
- 1 tablespoon tomato paste
- ½ cup chopped dry salami

Rinse and sort through beans. In a deep 3½- to 4-quart pan, bring water to a boil over high heat. Add beans. Let water return to a boil; then boil, uncovered, for 2 minutes. Remove pan from heat, cover, and let stand for 1 hour. Drain and rinse beans, discarding cooking water.

While beans are standing, in a 4-quart or larger electric slow cooker, combine onion, carrot, bell pepper, garlic, ham, bay leaf, thyme, and baking soda. Rinse chicken, pat dry, and coat with flour. Add beans to cooker; distribute chicken pieces over beans, then pour in broth. Cover and cook at low setting until meat near thighbone is very tender when pierced and beans are very tender to bite (8 to 9 hours).

Gently stir in tomato, tomato paste, and salami. Increase cooker heat setting to high; cover and cook until mixture is heated through (20 to 25 more minutes). Makes 6 servings.

Per serving: 651 calories (50% from fat), 54 g protein, 27 g carbohydrates, 35 g total fat (11 g saturated), 168 mg cholesterol, 1,291 mg sodium

Chicken with Barley & Pecans

Preparation time: About 15 minutes
Cooking time: 6½ to 7 hours

As the hours of leisurely cooking pass, chewy pearl barley absorbs the rich flavors of chicken and mushrooms. Set off this wholesome supper dish with a topping of toasted pecans; serve steamed broccoli alongside.

- 1 medium-size onion, finely chopped
- 2 cloves garlic, minced or pressed
- 8 ounces mushrooms, sliced
- ¼ teaspoon *each* salt and dry thyme
- 1 cup pearl barley, rinsed and drained
- 8 skinless, boneless chicken thighs (about 1½ lbs. *total*)
- ⅛ teaspoon paprika
- 1 can (about 14½ oz.) chicken broth

- ¼ cup coarsely chopped pecans
   Chopped parsley

In a 3-quart or larger electric slow cooker, combine onion, garlic, mushrooms, salt, thyme, and barley. Rinse chicken, pat dry, and arrange over barley mixture. Sprinkle with paprika. Pour in broth. Cover and cook at low setting until chicken is very tender when pierced and barley is tender to bite (6½ to 7 hours).

When chicken is almost done, toast pecans in a small nonstick frying pan over medium heat until golden brown (5 to 8 minutes), stirring occasionally. Set aside.

To serve, sprinkle chicken and barley with pecans and parsley. Makes 4 servings.

Per serving: 460 calories (25% from fat), 42 g protein, 45 g carbohydrates, 13 g total fat (2 g saturated), 141 mg cholesterol, 736 mg sodium

Cranberry Chicken

Preparation time: About 10 minutes

Cooking time: 6¾ to 7¾ hours

Bright cranberries, fresh or frozen, give this appealing dish its sparkle. (There's no need to thaw frozen berries before using them.)

- 1 **small onion, thinly sliced**
- 1 **cup fresh or frozen (unthawed) cranberries**
- 12 **skinless, boneless chicken thighs (about 2¼ lbs. *total*)**
- ¼ **cup catsup**
- 2 **tablespoons firmly packed brown sugar**
- 1 **teaspoon dry mustard**
- 2 **teaspoons cider vinegar**
- 1½ **tablespoons cornstarch blended with 2 tablespoons cold water**
  Salt

In a 3-quart or larger electric slow cooker, combine onion and cranberries. Rinse chicken, pat dry, and arrange on top of cranberry mixture. In a small bowl, mix catsup, sugar, mustard, and vinegar; pour over chicken. Cover and cook at low setting until chicken is very tender when pierced (6½ to 7½ hours).

Carefully lift chicken to a warm serving dish and keep warm. Blend cornstarch mixture into cooking liquid. Increase cooker heat setting to high; cover and cook, stirring 2 or 3 times, until sauce is thickened (10 to 15 more minutes). Season sauce to taste with salt; pour over chicken. Makes 6 servings.

Per serving: 251 calories (25% from fat), 34 g protein, 12 g carbohydrates, 7 g total fat (2 g saturated), 141 mg cholesterol, 267 mg sodium

Saucy Chicken with Polenta

Preparation time: About 20 minutes

Cooking time: 6 to 7 hours

While the chicken simmers in a simple tomato-herb sauce, prepare a casserole of polenta and slip it into the oven to bake. Complete the meal with green beans and crusty rolls.

- 1 **small onion, finely chopped**
- 2 **cloves garlic, minced or pressed**
- ¼ **cup finely chopped green bell pepper**
- 2 **medium-size pear-shaped (Roma-type) tomatoes, seeded and chopped**
- 1 **teaspoon *each* dry oregano and dry basil**
- 8 **skinless, boneless chicken thighs (about 1½ lbs. *total*)**
- 1 **can (about 8 oz.) tomato sauce**
- ¼ **cup dry red wine**
- 1 **tablespoon cornstarch**
  Baked Polenta (recipe follows)
  Salt
  Italian parsley sprigs or chopped Italian parsley

In a 3-quart or larger electric slow cooker, combine onion, garlic, bell pepper, tomatoes, oregano, and basil. Rinse chicken, pat dry, and arrange on top of onion mixture. In a small bowl, mix tomato sauce, wine, and cornstarch; pour over chicken. Cover and cook at low setting until chicken is very tender when pierced (6 to 7 hours). About 45 minutes before chicken is done, prepare Baked Polenta.

To serve, lift chicken from sauce and arrange over polenta. Season sauce to taste with salt. Spoon a little of the sauce over chicken and polenta; serve remaining sauce in a bowl or pitcher. Garnish chicken with parsley. Makes 4 servings.

Baked Polenta. In a greased shallow 2-quart casserole, mix 3½ cups **chicken broth**, 1 cup **polenta** (Italian-style cornmeal), and 1 tablespoon **olive oil**. Bake in a 350° oven until broth has been absorbed (40 to 45 minutes). Sprinkle with ¼ cup grated **Parmesan cheese.**

Per serving: 452 calories (27% from fat), 43 g protein, 39 g carbohydrates, 14 g total fat (3 g saturated), 145 mg cholesterol, 1,453 mg sodium

Chicken with Apricots & Olives

Preparation time: About 15 minutes
Cooking time: 6¼ to 7¼ hours

Orzo or hot steamed rice makes a nice foil for this bold-flavored dish. A sweet-tart sauce cloaks plump apricots, pungent Niçoise olives, and tender chicken legs.

⅓   **cup dried apricots**
⅓   **cup drained Niçoise or calamata olives**
2   **cloves garlic, minced or pressed**
½   **teaspoon grated orange peel**
1   **tablespoon dry basil**
4   **whole chicken legs (about 2 lbs. *total*)**
    Freshly ground pepper
2   **tablespoons *each* drained capers and firmly packed brown sugar**
¼   **cup *each* orange juice and white wine vinegar**
    Orange slices and Italian parsley sprigs

In a 4-quart or larger electric slow cooker, combine apricots, olives, garlic, orange peel, and basil. Rinse chicken and pat dry; then arrange on top of apricot mixture. Sprinkle with pepper, capers, and sugar; drizzle with orange juice and vinegar. Cover and cook at low setting until meat near thighbone is very tender when pierced (6 to 7 hours).

Carefully lift chicken to a warm serving dish; using a slotted spoon, lift apricots and olives from cooker and arrange around chicken. Keep warm. Skim and discard fat from cooking liquid; pour liquid into a small pan. Bring to a boil over high heat; then boil, stirring often, until reduced to ½ cup (about 10 minutes). Pour sauce over chicken. Garnish with orange slices and parsley sprigs. Makes 4 servings.

Per serving: 343 calories (43% from fat), 31 g protein, 18 g carbohydrates, 24 g total fat (4 g saturated), 131 mg cholesterol, 635 mg sodium

Chile-Orange Chicken

Preparation time: About 15 minutes
Cooking time: 6¼ to 7¼ hours

Chunks of chicken thigh simmer in an unusual, spicy orange sauce, its flavor deepened with unsweetened cocoa. You might serve meat and sauce over brown rice.

2   **pounds skinless, boneless chicken thighs**
1   **small onion, finely chopped**
2   **cloves garlic, minced or pressed**
2   **teaspoons grated orange peel**
1   **tablespoon ground dried New Mexico or California chiles**
1   **tablespoon unsweetened cocoa**
½   **teaspoon *each* sugar and ground cinnamon**
1   **teaspoon ground cumin**
⅓   **cup orange juice**
¼   **cup cream sherry**
1½   **tablespoons cornstarch blended with 2 tablespoons cold water**
    Salt
    Orange slices

Rinse chicken, pat dry, and cut into 1½-inch chunks. In a 3-quart or larger electric slow cooker, combine chicken, onion, garlic, orange peel, chiles, cocoa, sugar, cinnamon, and cumin; mix lightly. Pour in orange juice and sherry. Cover and cook at low setting until chicken is very tender when pierced (6 to 7 hours).

Skim and discard fat from cooking liquid, if necessary; then blend in cornstarch mixture. Increase cooker heat setting to high; cover and cook, stirring 2 or 3 times, until sauce is thickened (about 10 more minutes). Season to taste with salt; garnish with orange slices. Makes 6 servings.

Per serving: 173 calories (11% from fat), 30 g protein, 7 g carbohydrates, 2 g total fat (0.4 g saturated), 122 mg cholesterol, 133 mg sodium

*Offer orzo or another small pasta to absorb the luscious sauce
of Chicken with Apricots & Olives (recipe on facing page). Tender-crisp
sugar snap peas provide a crunchy accent.*

Spanish Chicken

Preparation time: About 15 minutes
Cooking time: 6¼ to 7¼ hours

A splash of sherry wine lends a Spanish accent to chicken thighs braised with tiny whole onions and a savory blend of spices and herbs.

- 1 **small onion, finely chopped**
- 3 **cloves garlic, minced or pressed**
- 1 **package (about 10 oz.) frozen small white onions**
- ½ **teaspoon *each* ground coriander and dry thyme**
- 1 **dry bay leaf**
- 1 **small dried hot red chile**
- 6 **juniper berries**
- 1 **cinnamon stick (about 2 inches long)**
- 8 **skinless, boneless chicken thighs (about 1½ lbs. *total*)**
- 1 **tablespoon tomato paste**
- ¼ **cup *each* dry sherry and red wine vinegar**
- **Salt**
- **Chopped parsley**

In a 3-quart or larger electric slow cooker, combine chopped onion, garlic, frozen onions, coriander, thyme, bay leaf, chile, juniper berries, and cinnamon stick. Rinse chicken, pat dry, and arrange on top of onion mixture. In a small bowl, mix tomato paste, sherry, and vinegar; pour over chicken. Cover and cook at low setting until chicken is very tender when pierced (6 to 7 hours).

Carefully lift chicken and small onions to a warm serving bowl; keep warm. Strain cooking liquid into a small pan, discarding seasonings. Bring liquid to a boil over high heat; then boil, stirring often, until reduced to ½ cup (8 to 10 minutes). Season sauce to taste with salt, then pour over chicken. Sprinkle with parsley. Makes 4 servings.

Per serving: 260 calories (26% from fat), 35 g protein, 13 g carbohydrates, 7 g total fat (2 g saturated), 141 mg cholesterol, 189 mg sodium

Ginger Chicken Breasts with Bulgur

Preparation time: About 15 minutes
Cooking time: 6¼ to 7¼ hours

Cook chicken breasts in broth seasoned with cilantro, ginger, and soy; then simmer bulgur in the cooking liquid and serve it as a nutty-tasting base for the tender meat.

- ½ **cup lightly packed cilantro leaves**
- 2 **tablespoons grated fresh ginger**
- 3 **cloves garlic, minced or pressed**
- ¼ **cup thinly sliced green onions**
- 6 **skinless, boneless chicken breast halves (about 2 lbs. *total*)**
- 3 **tablespoons soy sauce**
- ½ **cup low-sodium chicken broth**
- 1 **cup bulgur (cracked wheat)**
- **Cilantro sprigs**

In a 4-quart or larger electric slow cooker, combine cilantro leaves, ginger, garlic, and 2 tablespoons of the onions. Rinse chicken and pat dry; then arrange, overlapping pieces slightly, on top of cilantro mixture. Pour soy sauce and broth over chicken. Cover and cook at low setting until chicken is very tender when pierced (6 to 7 hours).

Carefully lift chicken to a warm plate and keep warm. Stir bulgur into cooking liquid. Increase cooker heat setting to high; cover and cook until almost all liquid has been absorbed (15 to 20 more minutes).

To serve, spoon bulgur onto a warm platter; arrange chicken over bulgur. Sprinkle with remaining 2 tablespoons onions. Garnish with cilantro sprigs. Makes 6 servings.

Per serving: 259 calories (8% from fat), 39 g protein, 20 g carbohydrates, 2 g total fat (0.6 g saturated), 88 mg cholesterol, 623 mg sodium

Roman-style Chicken

Preparation time: About 15 minutes

Cooking time: 6½ to 7 hours

Shiny ripe olives dot the bright tomato sauce that coats these chicken legs. Serve with pasta or polenta (such as Baked Polenta, page 57) and steamed spinach or chard.

- 1 medium-size onion, thinly sliced
- 3 cloves garlic, thinly sliced
- 1 medium-size red bell pepper, seeded and thinly sliced
- 1 tablespoon dry rosemary
- 1 can (about 6 oz.) pitted ripe olives, drained
- 1 tablespoon drained capers
- 6 whole chicken legs (3 to 3½ lbs. *total*)
  Freshly ground pepper
- 1 large can (about 15 oz.) tomato sauce
  Salt

In a 4-quart or larger electric slow cooker, combine onion, garlic, bell pepper, rosemary, olives, and capers. Rinse chicken and pat dry; then arrange, overlapping pieces slightly, over bell pepper mixture. Sprinkle with pepper; pour in tomato sauce. Cover and cook at low setting until meat near thighbone is very tender when pierced (6½ to 7 hours).

Carefully lift chicken to a warm serving dish. Skim and discard fat from sauce; season sauce to taste with salt, then spoon over chicken. Makes 6 servings.

Per serving: 354 calories (50% from fat), 34 g protein, 10 g carbohydrates, 20 g total fat (5 g saturated), 144 mg cholesterol, 855 mg sodium

Rosemary & Red Pepper Chicken Breasts

Preparation time: About 20 minutes

Cooking time: 6¼ to 7¼ hours

In Italy, spirited chicken dishes like this one are sometimes known as *pollo alla contadina* —"peasant-style chicken." Serve with pasta strands such as fettuccine or linguine.

- 1 small onion, thinly sliced
- 1 medium-size red bell pepper, seeded and cut into thin bite-size strips
- 4 cloves garlic, minced or pressed
- 2 teaspoons dry rosemary
- ½ teaspoon dry oregano
- 8 ounces mild turkey Italian sausages, casings removed
- 8 skinless, boneless chicken breast halves (2¼ to 2½ lbs. *total*)
- ¼ teaspoon coarsely ground pepper
- ¼ cup dry vermouth
- 1½ tablespoons cornstarch blended with 2 tablespoons cold water
  Salt
  Chopped parsley

In a 4-quart or larger electric slow cooker, combine onion, bell pepper, garlic, rosemary, and oregano. Crumble sausages over onion mixture. Rinse chicken and pat dry; then arrange, overlapping pieces slightly, over sausage mixture. Sprinkle with pepper; pour in vermouth. Cover and cook at low setting until chicken is very tender when pierced (6 to 7 hours).

Lift chicken to a warm deep platter and keep warm. Blend cornstarch mixture into cooking liquid. Increase cooker heat setting to high; cover and cook, stirring 2 or 3 times, until sauce is thickened (about 10 more minutes). Season sauce to taste with salt; spoon over chicken. Sprinkle with parsley. Makes 8 servings.

Per serving: 209 calories (21% from fat), 36 g protein, 4 g carbohydrates, 5 g total fat (0.4 g saturated), 98 mg cholesterol, 286 mg sodium

*After Country Captain Chicken Breasts (recipe on facing page) have
simmered for hours, you add rice and shrimp to cook in the spicy, richly
flavored broth. Serve the colorful dish with a butter lettuce salad,
flaky baking powder biscuits, and iced tea.*

Chicken Breasts Calvados

Preparation time: About 10 minutes

Cooking time: 6¼ to 7¼ hours

Elegant enough for a small dinner party, this easy-to-prepare dish of chicken and sweet apples features a topping of bubbly melted cheese and a sauce flavored with apple brandy. Pour a fruity Gewürztraminer or Chenin Blanc to sip with the meal.

    2 medium-size Golden Delicious apples,
       peeled, cored, and sliced
    4 large skinless, boneless chicken breast
       halves (about 1½ lbs. *total*)
       Salt and freshly ground white pepper
    ½ teaspoon ground nutmeg
    ¼ cup apple brandy, brandy, or apple juice
    4 slices Havarti cheese (about 1 oz. *each*)
       Chopped parsley

Spread apples in a 3-quart or larger electric slow cooker. Rinse chicken and pat dry; then arrange, overlapping pieces slightly, on top of apples. Sprinkle with salt, white pepper, and nutmeg; pour in brandy. Cover; cook at low setting until chicken is very tender when pierced (6 to 7 hours).

Lift chicken to a shallow 1½-quart baking dish; using a slotted spoon, lift apples from cooker and arrange around chicken. Pour cooking liquid into a small pan, bring to a boil over high heat, and boil, stirring often, until liquid is reduced to ⅓ cup (8 to 10 minutes). Pour liquid over chicken. Cover each chicken piece with a slice of cheese. Broil about 6 inches below heat until cheese is bubbly and lightly browned (about 2 minutes). Sprinkle with parsley. Makes 4 servings.

Per serving: 326 calories (10% from fat), 46 g protein, 11 g carbohydrates, 10 g total fat (5 g saturated), 128 mg cholesterol, 324 mg sodium

Pictured on facing page

Country Captain Chicken Breasts

Preparation time: About 30 minutes

Cooking time: 6¾ to 7¾ hours

The distinctive combination of curry, ginger, and fruit gives this classic Southern dish its character.

    2 medium-size Granny Smith apples
    1 small onion, finely chopped
    1 small green bell pepper, seeded and finely
       chopped
    3 cloves garlic, minced or pressed
    2 tablespoons dried currants
    1 tablespoon curry powder
    1 teaspoon ground ginger
    ¼ teaspoon ground red pepper (cayenne)
    1 can (about 14¼ oz.) diced tomatoes
    6 small skinless, boneless chicken breast halves
       (about 1¾ lbs. *total*)
    ½ cup chicken broth
    1 cup long-grain white rice
    1 pound large raw shrimp, shelled and deveined
    ⅓ cup slivered almonds
       Salt
       Chopped parsley

Quarter, core, and dice unpeeled apples. In a 4-quart or larger electric slow cooker, combine apples, onion, bell pepper, garlic, currants, curry powder, ginger, and red pepper; stir in tomatoes. Rinse chicken and pat dry; then arrange, overlapping pieces slightly, on top of tomato mixture. Pour in broth. Cover and cook at low setting until chicken is very tender when pierced (6 to 7 hours).

Carefully lift chicken to a warm plate, cover lightly, and keep warm in a 200° oven. Stir rice into cooking liquid. Increase cooker heat setting to high; cover and cook, stirring once or twice, until rice is almost tender to bite (30 to 35 minutes). Stir in shrimp, cover, and cook until shrimp are opaque in center; cut to test (about 10 more minutes).

Meanwhile, toast almonds in a small nonstick frying pan over medium heat until golden brown (5 to 8 minutes), stirring occasionally. Set aside.

To serve, season rice mixture to taste with salt. Mound in a warm serving dish; arrange chicken on top. Sprinkle with parsley and almonds. Makes 6 servings.

Per serving: 429 calories (16% from fat), 48 g protein, 41 g carbohydrates, 7 g total fat (1 g saturated), 170 mg cholesterol, 375 mg sodium

Costa Rican Turkey with Rice

Preparation time: About 20 minutes
Cooking time: 8¾ to 10¾ hours

The lilting flavors of this Central American dish are deliciously complemented by black beans, warm corn tortillas, and a mixed green salad.

- 1 turkey breast half (2 to 2½ lbs.)
- 1 large onion, finely chopped
- 2 cloves garlic, minced or pressed
- 1 large can (about 7 oz.) diced green chiles
- 2 medium-size tomatoes, peeled, seeded, and chopped
- 2 tablespoons drained capers
- 1 teaspoon ground cumin
- ½ teaspoon dry oregano
- 1½ cups chicken broth
- 1¼ cups short-grain white rice
- ¼ cup lightly packed cilantro leaves
- Salt

Rinse turkey, pat dry, and place in a 4-quart or larger electric slow cooker. Distribute onion, garlic, chiles, and tomatoes over and around turkey. Sprinkle with capers, cumin, and oregano; pour in broth. Cover and cook at low setting until meat in thickest part is very tender when pierced (8 to 10 hours).

Carefully lift out turkey and let stand until cool enough to handle. Meanwhile, skim and discard fat from cooking liquid; then stir in rice. Increase cooker heat setting to high; cover and cook, stirring once or twice, until rice is almost tender to bite (30 to 35 minutes).

Remove and discard skin and bones from turkey; cut or tear meat into bite-size pieces. Stir turkey and cilantro into rice mixture; cover and cook until heated through (about 10 more minutes). Season to taste with salt. Makes 6 to 8 servings.

Per serving: 288 calories (5% from fat), 32 g protein, 34 g carbohydrates, 1 g total fat (0.3 g saturated), 72 mg cholesterol, 509 mg sodium

Turkey Breast Braised with Cider & Apples

Preparation time: About 20 minutes
Cooking time: 8¼ to 10¼ hours

Spiced apples bring sweet, sophisticated flavor to this appealing meat-and-potatoes combination.

- 3 shallots, thinly sliced
- 6 small thin-skinned potatoes (*each* about 2 inches in diameter), scrubbed and cut lengthwise into quarters
- 1 dry bay leaf
- 2 medium-size tart green apples, peeled, cored, and cut into eighths
- 1 boneless, skinless turkey breast half (2 to 2½ lbs.), rolled and tied
- ¼ teaspoon *each* ground white pepper and ground nutmeg
- ⅛ teaspoon ground cinnamon
- ½ cup apple cider or apple juice
- 1½ tablespoons cornstarch blended with 2 tablespoons cold water
- Salt
- Chopped parsley

In a 4-quart or larger electric slow cooker, combine shallots, potatoes, and bay leaf. Arrange apples over potato mixture. Rinse turkey, pat dry, and place on top of apples; sprinkle with white pepper, nutmeg, and cinnamon. Pour in cider. Cover and cook at low setting until meat in thickest part is very tender when pierced (8 to 10 hours).

Carefully lift turkey to a warm serving dish. Using a slotted spoon, lift out apples and potatoes and arrange around turkey. Keep warm. Blend cornstarch mixture into cooking liquid. Increase cooker heat setting to high; cover and cook, stirring 2 or 3 times, until sauce is thickened (12 to 15 more minutes). Season sauce to taste with salt.

To serve, slice turkey about ¼ inch thick. Spoon some of the sauce over turkey slices, apples, and potatoes; sprinkle with parsley. Serve remaining sauce in a bowl or pitcher to add to taste. Makes 6 servings.

Per serving: 273 calories (5% from fat), 41 g protein, 22 g carbohydrates, 1 g total fat (0.4 g saturated), 100 mg cholesterol, 85 mg sodium

Smoky Turkey Stew

Preparation time: About 20 minutes

Cooking time: 8¼ to 10¼ hours

Here's an especially good filling for soft tacos: turkey cooked to tenderness in a smoky-tasting, spicy-sweet sauce.

- 1 large onion, finely chopped
- 3 cloves garlic, minced or pressed
- ⅓ cup firmly packed brown sugar
- 1 tablespoon chili powder
- 1 teaspoon *each* dry mustard and instant coffee powder
- 2 turkey thighs (3 to 3½ lbs. *total*), skinned
- 1 large can (about 15 oz.) tomato sauce
- 2 tablespoons *each* tomato paste, lime juice, and red wine vinegar
- ⅛ teaspoon liquid smoke
  Salt

In a 4-quart or larger electric slow cooker, combine onion, garlic, sugar, chili powder, mustard, and coffee powder. Rinse turkey, pat dry, and place on top of onion mixture. In a bowl, mix tomato sauce, tomato paste, lime juice, vinegar, and liquid smoke; pour over turkey. Cover and cook at low setting until turkey is so tender it pulls from bones when prodded with a fork (8 to 10 hours).

Carefully lift out turkey and let stand until cool enough to handle. Meanwhile, skim and discard fat from cooking liquid; pour liquid into a 3-quart pan. Bring to a boil over medium-high heat; then boil, stirring often, until reduced to about 2½ cups (about 10 minutes).

Meanwhile, remove and discard bones and fat from turkey; tear meat into bite-size pieces. Stir turkey into hot cooking liquid; reduce heat to low and cook, stirring gently once or twice, until heated through (about 5 more minutes). Season to taste with salt. Makes 6 to 8 servings.

Per serving: 209 calories (15% from fat), 26 g protein, 19 g carbohydrates, 4 g total fat (1 g saturated), 88 mg cholesterol, 516 mg sodium

Braised Turkey Drumsticks

Preparation time: About 15 minutes

Cooking time: 8½ to 10½ hours

This simple turkey-vegetable stew has an appealing old-fashioned flavor. Try it on a cold day, with baked potatoes to soak up the sauce.

- 1 medium-size onion, thinly sliced
- 2 stalks celery, cut into thin slanting slices
- 4 medium-size carrots, cut into ¼-inch-thick slanting slices
- 2 cloves garlic, minced or pressed
- ¼ teaspoon *each* dry thyme and celery seeds
- 4 medium-size turkey drumsticks (3½ to 4 lbs. *total*)
  Freshly ground pepper
- ½ cup dry white wine
- 2 tablespoons cornstarch blended with 2 tablespoons cold water
  Salt
  Chopped parsley

In a 5-quart or larger electric slow cooker, combine onion, celery, carrots, garlic, thyme, and celery seeds. Rinse turkey, pat dry, and arrange over onion mixture. Sprinkle with pepper; pour in wine. Cover and cook at low setting until turkey is so tender it pulls away from bones when prodded with a fork (8 to 10 hours).

Carefully lift out turkey and let stand until cool enough to handle. Meanwhile, skim and discard fat from cooking liquid, then blend in cornstarch mixture. Increase cooker heat setting to high; cover and cook, stirring 2 or 3 times, until sauce is thickened (10 to 15 more minutes).

Remove and discard skin, bones, and tendons from turkey; tear meat into large chunks and stir into sauce. Cover and cook until heated through (about 10 more minutes). Season to taste with salt. Sprinkle with parsley. Makes 6 servings.

Per serving: 238 calories (4% from fat), 45 g protein, 9 g carbohydrates, 1 g total fat (0.5 g saturated), 179 mg cholesterol, 185 mg sodium

Herbed Turkey Roast

Preparation time: About 20 minutes
Cooking time: 9¼ to 10¼ hours

When sliced, this flavorful stuffed turkey breast reveals a heart of green herbs and pink prosciutto.

- 1 **whole turkey breast (4 to 5 lbs.), boned**
- ¼ **cup chopped parsley**
- 2 **tablespoons minced fresh thyme or 2 teaspoons dry thyme**
  Salt and pepper
- 2 **ounces** *each* **thinly sliced fontina cheese and prosciutto**
- 3 **or 4 thyme or parsley sprigs** (*each* **3 to 4 inches long**)
- ⅔ **cup chicken broth**
- ⅓ **cup dry white wine**
- 2 **tablespoons cornstarch blended with 2 tablespoons cold water**
  Additional thyme or parsley sprigs (optional)

Rinse turkey, pat dry, and place, skin side down, on a board. Sprinkle meat side of turkey with

chopped parsley and minced thyme; season to taste with salt and pepper. Cover with cheese and prosciutto, overlapping slices. Starting with a long edge, roll up turkey firmly, jelly roll style. Overlap 3 or 4 thyme sprigs down length of roll; tie roll securely with string at 2-inch intervals. (At this point, you may cover and refrigerate until next day.)

Place turkey roll, thyme side up, in a 4-quart or larger electric slow cooker. Pour in broth and wine. Cover and cook at low setting until meat in thickest part is very tender when pierced (9 to 10 hours).

Carefully lift turkey to a warm platter and keep warm. Skim and discard fat from cooking liquid, if necessary; blend in cornstarch mixture. Increase cooker heat setting to high; cover and cook, stirring 2 or 3 times, until sauce is thickened (10 to 15 more minutes).

Remove and discard strings and thyme sprigs from turkey; slice meat ¼ inch thick. Garnish with additional thyme sprigs, if desired; serve with sauce to add to taste. Makes 10 to 12 servings.

Per serving: 300 calories (43% from fat), 39 g protein, 2 g carbohydrates, 14 g total fat (4 g saturated), 117 mg cholesterol, 267 mg sodium

Curried Turkey with Currants

Preparation time: About 25 minutes
Cooking time: 8¼ to 10¼ hours

Tomatoes and red bell pepper bring a tart-sweet flavor and a rosy hue to this mild curry. Serve it with hot cooked rice, either brown or white.

- 1 **large onion, thinly sliced**
- 1 **medium-size red bell pepper, seeded and thinly sliced**
- 2 **cloves garlic, minced or pressed**
- 1 **tablespoon curry powder**
- ¼ **teaspoon ground red pepper (cayenne)**
- ½ **cup dried currants**
- 2 **turkey thighs (3 to 3½ lbs.** *total***), skinned**
- 1 **can (about 14½ oz.) diced tomatoes**
- 2 **tablespoons cornstarch blended with 2 tablespoons cold water**
  Salt
- ¼ **cup chopped roasted salted almonds**

In a 4-quart or larger electric slow cooker, combine onion, bell pepper, garlic, curry powder, red pepper, and currants. Rinse turkey, pat dry, and arrange on top of onion mixture. Pour in tomatoes and their liquid. Cover and cook at low setting until turkey is so tender it pulls from bones when prodded with a fork (8 to 10 hours).

Carefully lift out turkey and let stand until cool enough to handle. Meanwhile, skim and discard fat from cooking liquid, if necessary; then blend in cornstarch mixture. Increase cooker heat setting to high; cover and cook, stirring 2 or 3 times, until sauce is thickened (about 15 more minutes).

Remove and discard bones and fat from turkey; tear meat into bite-size pieces and stir into sauce. Season to taste with salt; sprinkle with almonds. Makes 8 servings.

Per serving: 195 calories (23% from fat), 23 g protein, 14 g carbohydrates, 5 g total fat (1 g saturated), 76 mg cholesterol, 208 mg sodium

Make our prosciutto-stuffed Herbed Turkey Roast (recipe on facing page) the centerpiece of a worry-free Christmas feast. While the turkey simmers in the slow cooker, you can enjoy all the day's festivities.

Turkey Mole

Preparation time: About 30 minutes

Cooking time: 8¾ to 10¾ hours

This greatly simplified version of a classic Mexican dish is nonetheless authentic in flavor. Serve it with rice and steamy-hot corn tortillas.

- ¼ cup sesame seeds
- ½ cup slivered almonds
- 1 dried New Mexico or California chile
- 1 large onion, chopped
- 3 cloves garlic, crushed
- ⅓ cup raisins
- 2 tablespoons chili powder
- ½ teaspoon ground coriander
- ¼ teaspoon ground cloves
- ¼ teaspoon anise seeds, coarsely crushed
- 1 cinnamon stick (about 2 inches long)
- 3½ to 4 pounds turkey thighs
- 1 can (about 14½ oz.) diced tomatoes
- ¼ cup *each* tomato paste and tequila
- 1 ounce unsweetened chocolate, coarsely chopped
  Salt

Toast sesame seeds in a small nonstick frying pan over medium heat until golden brown (3 to 5 minutes), stirring often; remove from pan. Add almonds to pan and toast until golden brown (5 to 8 minutes), stirring occasionally; remove from pan. Add chile to pan and cook, turning occasionally, until chile is softened and richly fragrant (about 2 minutes); remove from pan.

In a 5-quart or larger electric slow cooker, combine onion, garlic, raisins, chili powder, coriander, cloves, anise seeds, cinnamon stick, chile, almonds, and sesame seeds. Rinse turkey, pat dry, and place in cooker. Pour in tomatoes. Mix tomato paste and tequila; pour over turkey. Cover and cook at low setting until turkey is so tender it pulls away from bones when prodded with a fork (8½ to 10½ hours).

Lift out turkey and let stand until cool enough to handle. Skim and discard fat from cooking liquid; remove and discard cinnamon stick and stem of chile. Pour cooking liquid into a blender or food processor and whirl until smooth; return to cooker and increase heat setting to high. Stir in chocolate, cover, and cook, stirring once or twice, until chocolate is melted (about 5 minutes).

Remove and discard skin, bones, and fat from turkey; add meat (in large chunks) to sauce. Cover and cook until heated through (about 10 more minutes). Season to taste with salt. Makes 6 to 8 servings.

Per serving: 276 calories (28% from fat), 33 g protein, 19 g carbohydrates, 9 g total fat (2 g saturated), 97 mg cholesterol, 307 mg sodium

Turkey Ragout

Preparation time: About 20 minutes

Cooking time: 7½ to 8½ hours

We started with a favorite stew recipe, then replaced the veal called for in the original with lean, juicy turkey breast. Serve with your favorite small pasta.

- 1 large onion, thinly sliced
- 2 cloves garlic, minced or pressed
- 8 ounces mushrooms, cut into quarters
- ½ teaspoon dry thyme
- ⅛ teaspoon ground white pepper
- 2 pounds boneless, skinless turkey breast
- 3 tablespoons all-purpose flour
- ⅓ cup dry white wine or chicken broth
- 1 tablespoon tomato paste
  Salt

In a 3-quart or larger electric slow cooker, combine onion, garlic, mushrooms, thyme, and white pepper. Rinse turkey, pat dry, and cut into 1½-inch cubes. Coat turkey cubes with flour; arrange on top of onion mixture. Mix wine and tomato paste; pour over turkey. Cover and cook at low setting until turkey is very tender when pierced (7½ to 8½ hours). Stir gently to coat turkey with sauce, then season to taste with salt. Makes 6 servings.

Per serving: 206 calories (6% from fat), 39 g protein, 8 g carbohydrates, 1 g total fat (0.3 g saturated), 94 mg cholesterol, 99 mg sodium

All-day Turkey Spaghetti

Preparation time: About 20 minutes

Cooking time: 8½ to 10½ hours

To make this rich, red pasta sauce, you use just the meatier turkey wing joints. (If you buy whole turkey wings, reserve the bony tips for soup stock.)

- 1   medium-size onion, finely chopped
- 1   red bell pepper, seeded and chopped
- 3   cloves garlic, minced or pressed
- 1   medium-size carrot, shredded
- 8   ounces mushrooms, sliced
- 2   tablespoons dried currants
- 1   tablespoon Italian herb seasoning; or ¾ teaspoon *each* dry basil, marjoram, oregano, and thyme
- 2   mild turkey Italian sausages (about 6 oz. *total*), casings removed
- 3   to 3½ pounds meaty turkey wings
- 1   can (about 15 oz.) tomato purée
- ½   cup dry red wine
- 2   tablespoons balsamic vinegar
      Salt and pepper
- 1   pound dry spaghetti, cooked and drained
      Grated Parmesan cheese (optional)

In a 3½-quart or larger electric slow cooker, combine onion, bell pepper, garlic, carrot, mushrooms, currants, and herb seasoning. Crumble sausages over vegetables. Rinse turkey, pat dry, and arrange on top of sausage mixture. In a small bowl, mix tomato purée and wine; pour over turkey. Cover and cook at low setting until turkey is so tender it pulls away from bones when prodded with a fork (8 to 10 hours).

Carefully lift out turkey and let stand until cool enough to handle. Meanwhile, skim and discard fat from sauce; pour sauce into a 3-quart pan. Bring to a boil over medium-high heat; then boil, stirring often, until reduced to 3 cups (12 to 15 minutes). Stir in vinegar; then season to taste with salt and pepper.

Discard skin and bones from turkey; stir meat into sauce. Reduce heat to low and simmer until heated through (about 5 more minutes).

To serve, divide spaghetti among wide, shallow bowls; top with sauce. Offer cheese to add to taste, if desired. Makes 6 to 8 servings.

Per serving: 424 calories (13% from fat), 29 g protein, 62 g carbohydrates, 6 g total fat (0.8 g saturated), 56 mg cholesterol, 485 mg sodium

Soy-simmered Turkey Legs

Preparation time: About 15 minutes

Cooking time: 8¼ to 10¼ hours

This zesty combination of turkey, onion, and bell pepper is good with Chinese noodles.

- 1   medium-size onion, finely chopped
- 1   medium-size red bell pepper, seeded and chopped
- 3   cloves garlic, thinly sliced
- 1   small dried hot red chile
- ⅓   cup raisins
- 4   medium-size turkey drumsticks (3½ to 4 lbs. *total*)
- ½   cup dry sherry
- ¼   cup soy sauce
- 2   tablespoons cornstarch blended with 2 tablespoons cold water

In a 5-quart or larger electric slow cooker, combine onion, bell pepper, garlic, chile, and raisins. Rinse turkey, pat dry, and arrange on onion mixture. Pour in sherry and soy sauce. Cover; cook at low setting until turkey is so tender it pulls away from bones when prodded with a fork (8 to 10 hours).

Carefully lift turkey to a warm large serving dish; keep warm. Skim and discard fat from cooking liquid. Remove and discard chile, if desired. Blend in cornstarch mixture. Increase cooker heat setting to high; cover and cook, stirring 2 or 3 times, until sauce is thickened (about 10 more minutes). Pour sauce over turkey.

To serve, spoon meat away from bones; accompany with a spoonful of sauce. Makes 6 servings.

Per serving: 369 calories (30% from fat), 48 g protein, 16 g carbohydrates, 12 g total fat (4 g saturated), 163 mg cholesterol, 865 mg sodium

Toasting ground chiles with herbs and spices brings rich flavor
to meatless Spicy Black Bean Chili (recipe on page 72). Dress up each bowlful
with shredded jack cheese, a dollop of sour cream, and accents
of green onion and lime.

VEGETARIAN ENTRÉES

C rockery cooking is well suited to many of the foods central to a vegetarian regime. In the following pages, you'll find inventive and nourishing recipes based on dried beans, lentils, pasta, whole grains, and potatoes. Served with a crusty whole wheat loaf and a leafy salad, any of these dishes makes a satisfying repast.

Spicy Black Bean Chili

Preparation time: About 1 hour (including standing time)
Cooking time: 10½ to 12½ hours

This slow-cooker chili is adapted from a contemporary classic—the meatless black bean chili that attained gastronomic fame at Greens, a vegetarian restaurant at Fort Mason in San Francisco.

1 pound dried black beans
2 quarts plus 3 cups water
2 tablespoons cumin seeds
4 teaspoons dry oregano
1 tablespoon sweet Hungarian paprika
2 tablespoons ground dried pasilla or New Mexico chiles
1 large onion, finely chopped
1 green bell pepper, seeded and finely chopped
5 cloves garlic, minced or pressed
1 dry bay leaf
¼ teaspoon baking soda
1 can (about 14½ oz.) diced tomatoes
¼ cup lightly packed cilantro leaves
1½ to 2 cups (6 to 8 oz.) shredded jack cheese
Condiments (optional): Sour cream, sliced green onions, lime wedges, cilantro sprigs

Rinse and sort through beans. In a deep 3½- to 4-quart pan, bring 2 quarts of the water to a boil over high heat. Add beans. Let water return to a boil; then boil, uncovered, for 2 minutes. Remove pan from heat, cover, and let stand for 1 hour. Drain and rinse beans, discarding cooking water.

In a small nonstick frying pan, combine cumin seeds, oregano, paprika, and ground chiles; cook over medium heat, stirring, until paprika darkens and cumin seeds become fragrant (3 to 5 minutes). Remove from heat and set aside.

In a 3½-quart or larger electric slow cooker, combine onion, bell pepper, garlic, and bay leaf; sprinkle with paprika mixture and baking soda. Add beans to cooker; pour in remaining 3 cups water. Cover and cook at low setting until beans are very tender to bite (10 to 12 hours).

Stir in tomatoes. Increase cooker heat setting to high; cover and cook until chili is heated through (about 30 more minutes). Stir in cilantro. For each serving, place ¼ cup of the cheese in a wide, shallow bowl; ladle in chili. Serve with condiments to add to taste, if desired. Makes 6 to 8 servings.

Per serving: 371 calories (25% from fat), 23 g protein, 49 g carbohydrates, 11 g total fat (0.3 g saturated), 25 mg cholesterol, 285 mg sodium

California Hoppin' John

Preparation time: About 1 hour (including standing time)
Cooking time: 10 to 11 hours

Our Western-style version of a famous Southern dish adds chiles, cumin, and fresh tomatoes to the traditional black-eyed peas and rice.

1 pound dried black-eyed peas
2 quarts plus 3 cups water
1 medium-size onion, finely chopped
3 cloves garlic, minced or pressed
1 large can (about 7 oz.) diced green chiles
2 teaspoons ground cumin
¼ teaspoon *each* pepper and baking soda
1 dried or canned chipotle chile
½ cup short-grain brown rice
3 large tomatoes, peeled and chopped
Salt

Rinse and sort through peas. In a deep 3½- to 4-quart pan, bring 2 quarts of the water to a boil over high heat. Add peas. Let water return to a boil; then boil, uncovered, for 2 minutes. Remove pan from heat, cover, and let stand for 1 hour. Drain and rinse peas, discarding cooking water.

In a 3½-quart or larger electric slow cooker, combine onion, garlic, green chiles, cumin, pepper, baking soda, and chipotle chile. Stir in peas; pour in remaining 3 cups water. Cover and cook at low setting until peas are tender to bite (9 to 10 hours).

Remove and discard chipotle chile; stir in rice and tomatoes. Increase cooker heat setting to high; cover and cook until rice is tender to bite (45 to 55 more minutes). Season to taste with salt. Serve in wide, shallow bowls. Makes 6 to 8 servings.

Per serving: 304 calories (5% from fat), 18 g protein, 57 g carbohydrates, 2 g total fat (0.3 g saturated), 0 mg cholesterol, 224 mg sodium

Garbanzo Curry

Preparation time: About 1 hour (including standing time)

Cooking time: 10½ to 12½ hours

This spicy vegetable stew tastes good with steamed spinach or a leafy fresh spinach salad.

- 1 **pound dried garbanzo beans**
- 2 **quarts plus 2 cups water**
- 1 **medium-size onion, finely chopped**
- 2 **stalks celery, thinly sliced**
- 1 **red bell pepper, seeded and finely chopped**
- 4 **cloves garlic, minced or pressed**
- 1½ **pounds small red thin-skinned potatoes (*each about 2 inches in diameter*), scrubbed and cut lengthwise into sixths**
- 1½ **tablespoons curry powder**
- ¼ **teaspoon *each* baking soda and ground red pepper (cayenne)**
- 1 **can (about 8 oz.) tomato sauce**
  Salt
- 4 **green onions, thinly sliced**

Rinse and sort through beans. In a deep 3½- to 4-quart pan, bring 2 quarts of the water to a boil over high heat. Add beans. Let water return to a boil; then boil, uncovered, for 2 minutes. Remove pan from heat, cover, and let stand for 1 hour. Drain and rinse beans, discarding cooking water.

While beans are standing, in a 4-quart or larger electric slow cooker, combine chopped onion, celery, bell pepper, garlic, potatoes, curry powder, baking soda, and red pepper. Stir in beans; pour in remaining 2 cups water. Cover and cook at low setting until beans are very tender to bite (10 to 12 hours). Stir curry gently once during final hour of cooking.

Stir in tomato sauce. Increase cooker heat setting to high; cover and cook until curry is heated through (20 to 30 more minutes). Season to taste with salt; sprinkle with green onions. Makes 6 to 8 servings.

Per serving: 344 calories (11% from fat), 16 g protein, 63 g carbohydrates, 4 g total fat (0.4 g saturated), 0 mg cholesterol, 261 mg sodium

Pasta with Lentils & Chard

Preparation time: About 20 minutes

Cooking time: 6¼ to 7¼ hours

Well-seasoned lentils combine with tart greens in this piquant pasta sauce. Combine the sauce—along with chunks of creamy Neufchâtel cheese—with hot cooked linguine to make a hearty entrée.

- 1 **bunch Swiss chard (12 to 14 oz.)**
- 1 **cup lentils, rinsed and drained**
- 1 **medium-size onion, finely chopped**
- 2 **cloves garlic, minced or pressed**
- 1 **teaspoon cumin seeds, coarsely crushed**
- ½ **teaspoon crushed red pepper flakes**
- ⅛ **teaspoon coarsely ground black pepper**
- 2 **cups water**
- 12 **ounces dry linguine**
  Salt
- 6 **ounces Neufchâtel cheese (at room temperature), diced**
  Grated Parmesan cheese (optional)

Rinse chard well. Trim off coarse stem ends; then cut stems crosswise into ¼-inch-wide strips and set aside. Cover chard leaves and refrigerate.

In a 3-quart or larger electric slow cooker, combine chard stems, lentils, onion, garlic, cumin seeds, red pepper flakes, and black pepper. Pour in water. Cover and cook at low setting until lentils are tender when mashed with a fork (6 to 7 hours).

Cut chard leaves crosswise into ½-inch-wide strips; stir into cooker. Increase heat setting to high; cover and cook until chard is wilted and bright green (about 15 more minutes). Meanwhile, in a 5- to 6-quart pan, cook linguine in 3 quarts boiling water just until tender to bite (10 to 12 minutes); or cook according to package directions. Drain well; pour into a warm wide 4-quart bowl.

Season lentil sauce to taste with salt. Add lentil sauce and Neufchâtel cheese to linguine; mix lightly to coat well. Offer Parmesan cheese to add to taste, if desired. Makes 6 servings.

Per serving: 411 calories (18% from fat), 20 g protein, 65 g carbohydrates, 8 g total fat (4 g saturated), 22 mg cholesterol, 242 mg sodium

Spiced Lentils in Pocket Bread

Preparation time: About 20 minutes
Cooking time: 6 to 7 hours

For a Sunday night sandwich supper, spoon this savory lentil filling—warm or at room temperature—into heated pita bread halves.

- 1 **cup lentils, rinsed and drained**
- 1 **medium-size carrot, shredded**
- ½ **cup finely chopped red bell pepper**
- 2 **cloves garlic, minced or pressed**
- 1 **dry bay leaf**
- 1 **small dried hot red chile**
- 1 **teaspoon ground cumin**
- 2 **cups water**
  Yogurt Sauce (recipe follows)
- 3 **tablespoons** *each* **olive oil and red wine vinegar**
- ½ **cup thinly sliced green onions**
- 2 **stalks celery, thinly sliced**

Salt and pepper
4 **pita breads (*each* about 6 inches in diameter), cut into halves and warmed**

In a 3-quart or larger electric slow cooker, combine lentils, carrot, bell pepper, garlic, bay leaf, chile, and cumin; pour in water. Cover and cook at low setting until lentils are tender when mashed with a fork (6 to 7 hours). Prepare Yogurt Sauce.

Drain lentil mixture, if necessary; remove and discard chile and bay leaf. Mix in oil and vinegar; stir in onions and celery. Season to taste with salt and pepper. To serve, spoon lentil mixture into pita bread halves; add Yogurt Sauce to taste. Makes 4 servings.

Yogurt Sauce. In a small bowl, mix 1 cup **plain lowfat or nonfat yogurt** and 2 tablespoons *each* **golden raisins** and chopped **fresh mint**.

Per serving: 502 calories (22% from fat), 23 g protein, 77 g carbohydrates, 12 g total fat (2 g saturated), 3 mg cholesterol, 435 mg sodium

Brown Rice & Vegetable Risotto

Preparation time: About 30 minutes
Cooking time: 4¾ to 5¼ hours

Pasta and risotto *primavera* —dishes enhanced by spring vegetables— have recently become popular. But as the following recipe shows, winter vegetables can be just as delicious an accent.

- 1½ **cups short-grain brown rice**
- 1 **medium-size onion, finely chopped**
- 2 **leeks (white and pale green parts only), thinly sliced**
- 1 **stalk celery, thinly sliced**
- 2 **medium-size pear-shaped (Roma-type) tomatoes, seeded and chopped**
- 6 **ounces mushrooms, sliced**
- 2 **medium-size carrots, thinly sliced**
- ¼ **teaspoon saffron threads, crushed; or ⅛ teaspoon ground saffron**
- 3 **cloves garlic, minced or pressed**
- 2 **cups water**
- ½ **cup dry white wine**
- 2 **cups lightly packed spinach leaves**
- ¼ **cup chopped parsley**
- 1 **tablespoon grated lemon peel**
- 1 **cup (about 5 oz.) grated Parmesan cheese**
  Salt and pepper

In a 3½-quart or larger electric slow cooker, combine rice, onion, leeks, celery, tomatoes, mushrooms, carrots, saffron, and 2 cloves of the garlic; pour in water and wine. Cover and cook at low setting until rice is tender to bite (4½ to 5 hours).

Cut spinach leaves into slivers; stir into risotto. Cover and cook until spinach is wilted and mixture is heated through (about 10 more minutes). Meanwhile, in a small bowl, mix parsley, lemon peel, and remaining 1 clove garlic. Stir ¾ cup of the cheese into risotto, then season to taste with salt and pepper.

To serve, sprinkle remaining ¼ cup cheese over risotto; add parsley mixture to taste. Makes 4 to 6 servings.

Per serving: 382 calories (16% from fat), 15 g protein, 67 g carbohydrates, 7 g total fat (3 g saturated), 13 mg cholesterol, 366 mg sodium

The convenient filling for Spiced Lentils in Pocket Bread (recipe on facing page) simmers in your crockery cooker while you're away. When you return, it's ready to enjoy—along with cherry tomatoes, cucumber spears, and a minty yogurt topping—for a quick supper.

Tofu & Spinach Manicotti

Preparation time: About 20 minutes

Cooking time: 4¼ to 6¼ hours

Big pasta shells, stuffed with a flavorful filling of spinach and tofu, simmer until tender in a wine-accented tomato sauce. Depending on the brand of manicotti you use, the cooking time will vary; test and taste after 4 hours, then continue to cook, if necessary.

- 1 medium-size onion, finely chopped
- 1 stalk celery, thinly sliced
- 3 cloves garlic, minced or pressed
- 2 teaspoons Italian herb seasoning; or ½ teaspoon *each* dry basil, marjoram, oregano, and thyme
- 1 pound soft tofu, rinsed and drained
- 1 package (about 10 oz.) frozen chopped spinach, thawed and squeezed dry
- ¼ cup grated Parmesan cheese
- ½ teaspoon salt
- ⅛ teaspoon pepper
- 12 dry manicotti shells (about 6 oz. *total*)
- 2 large cans (about 15 oz. *each*) tomato sauce
- ½ cup dry red wine
- 1 cup (about 4 oz.) shredded mozzarella cheese

In a 5-quart or larger electric slow cooker, combine onion, celery, garlic, and herb seasoning. In a large bowl, combine tofu, spinach, Parmesan cheese, salt, and pepper; mix well. Stuff manicotti with tofu filling.

Arrange filled manicotti in a single layer over onion mixture in cooker. In bowl you used for filling, mix tomato sauce and wine; pour over manicotti. Cover and cook at low setting until manicotti are tender when pierced and no raw, starchy flavor remains (4 to 6 hours).

Sprinkle with mozzarella cheese. Increase cooker heat setting to high; cover and cook until cheese is melted (about 15 more minutes). Makes 6 servings.

Per serving: 280 calories (25% from fat), 16 g protein, 38 g carbohydrates, 8 g total fat (3 g saturated), 17 mg cholesterol, 1,228 mg sodium

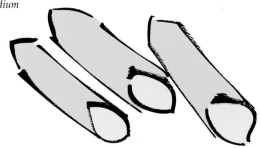

Barley, Mushroom & Cheese Pilaf

Preparation time: About 25 minutes

Cooking time: 6¼ to 7¼ hours

To complete this colorful dish, stir in chopped fresh broccoli when the barley is almost tender; then strew shredded sharp Cheddar over the top to melt.

- 1 medium-size onion, finely chopped
- 2 cloves garlic, minced or pressed
- 12 ounces mushrooms, sliced
- 3 medium-size carrots, cut into ¼-inch-thick slices
- ¼ teaspoon *each* salt, paprika, and dry rosemary
- 1 cup pearl barley, rinsed and drained
- 2 vegetable bouillon cubes
- 2 cups boiling water
- 1 cup tomato juice

    Salt
- 2 cups coarsely chopped broccoli
- 1 cup (about 4 oz.) shredded sharp Cheddar cheese

In a 3-quart or larger electric slow cooker, combine onion, garlic, mushrooms, carrots, salt, paprika, rosemary, and barley. Dissolve bouillon cubes in boiling water; pour bouillon and tomato juice over barley mixture. Cover and cook at low setting until barley is tender to bite and liquid is absorbed (6 to 7 hours).

Season barley mixture to taste with salt. Stir in broccoli; sprinkle with cheese. Increase cooker heat setting to high; cover and cook until broccoli is tender-crisp to bite and cheese is melted (about 15 more minutes). Makes 4 to 6 servings.

Per serving: 297 calories (25% from fat), 13 g protein, 45 g carbohydrates, 9 g total fat (5 g saturated), 24 mg cholesterol, 825 mg sodium

Potato & Artichoke Moussaka

Preparation time: About 30 minutes

Cooking time: 8¼ to 10¼ hours

Eggplant isn't usually a good candidate for inclusion in slow-cooker dishes. But if baked before going into the pot, it can make a delicious contribution to vegetable combinations like this one.

Olive oil cooking spray

1 medium-size eggplant (about 1 lb.), unpeeled, thinly sliced

2 jars (about 6 oz. *each*) marinated artichoke hearts

3 medium-size thin-skinned potatoes (1 to 1½ lbs. *total*)

1 tablespoon dry basil

2 cups (about 8 oz.) shredded Münster cheese

Spray a large, shallow-rimmed baking pan with cooking spray. Arrange eggplant slices in pan in a single layer. Drain artichoke hearts, reserving marinade; set artichokes aside. Brush eggplant with some of the marinade; reserve remaining marinade. Bake eggplant in a 425° oven until golden brown and soft when pressed (20 to 25 minutes).

Scrub potatoes well, but do not peel; then slice thinly. In a 3-quart or larger electric slow cooker, spread about a third of the potatoes to make bottom layer of moussaka. Sprinkle with 1 teaspoon of the basil, then layer on a third of the eggplant and a third of the artichokes. Repeat layers, using a third of the potatoes, basil, eggplant, and artichokes for each layer and ending with a layer of artichokes. Drizzle with reserved artichoke marinade.

Cover and cook at low setting until potatoes in center of mixture are very tender when pierced (8 to 10 hours). Sprinkle with cheese. Increase cooker heat setting to high; cover and cook until cheese is melted (about 15 more minutes). Makes 4 to 6 servings.

Per serving: 334 calories (50% from fat), 15 g protein, 28 g carbohydrates, 20 g total fat (9 g saturated), 44 mg cholesterol, 646 mg sodium

Green Chile, Cheddar & Potato Stew

Preparation time: About 20 minutes

Cooking time: 8½ to 10½ hours

This stew is really a hearty, chunky soup. Try it with thick slices of whole-grain bread or with warm whole wheat tortillas.

1 medium-size onion, thinly sliced

1 stalk celery, thinly sliced

2 medium-size pear-shaped (Roma-type) tomatoes, seeded and chopped

4 cloves garlic, minced or pressed

1 teaspoon *each* chili powder and ground cumin

½ teaspoon dry oregano

1 small can (about 4 oz.) diced green chiles

¼ cup lightly packed cilantro leaves

1½ pounds small thin-skinned potatoes (*each* about 2 inches in diameter), scrubbed and cut lengthwise into sixths

2 vegetable bouillon cubes

2 cups boiling water

Salt

1 cup (about 4 oz.) shredded sharp Cheddar cheese

Cilantro sprigs (optional)

In a 4-quart or larger electric slow cooker, combine onion, celery, tomatoes, garlic, chili powder, cumin, oregano, chiles, cilantro leaves, and potatoes. Dissolve bouillon cubes in boiling water; pour bouillon over potato mixture. Cover and cook at low setting until potatoes are very tender when pierced (8 to 10 hours).

Scoop out about 2 cups of the potatoes with a little of the liquid; whirl in a blender or food processor until puréed. Return purée to cooker. Increase heat setting to high; cover and cook until stew is heated through (about 20 more minutes). Season to taste with salt. Ladle into wide, shallow bowls; sprinkle evenly with cheese. Garnish with cilantro sprigs, if desired. Makes 4 servings.

Per serving: 292 calories (31% from fat), 12 g protein, 39 g carbohydrates, 10 g total fat (6 g saturated), 30 mg cholesterol, 844 mg sodium

For a bistro-style supper, complement quickly grilled lamb chops with slow-cooked Potato, Onion & Tomato Gratin (recipe on page 87). To round out the meal, offer a salad of endive spears and slivered beets, sprinkled with toasted walnuts and drizzled with vinaigrette dressing.

ACCOMPANIMENTS

N ot just for main dishes, the versatile slow cooker also turns out a

variety of accompaniments—and homey desserts, too. Like all our recipes, the

selections in this chapter offer a great way to beat the summer heat, since they let

you cook without turning on your oven.

o

A Trio of Roots

Preparation time: About 20 minutes

Cooking time: 8 to 10 hours

Honey and lemon lend a sweet-tart accent to this hearty combination of winter root vegetables, delicious with roast chicken or pork.

   2 **medium-size carrots, coarsely shredded**
   ¼ **cup chopped shallots**
   2 **medium-size russet potatoes (about 1 lb.** *total***),
      peeled and cut into ½-inch cubes**
   1 **medium-size celery root (about 12 oz.)**
   ¼ **cup chicken broth**
   2 **tablespoons lemon juice**
   1 **tablespoon honey**
   1 **tablespoon butter or margarine**
      Salt and pepper
      Chopped parsley

In a 3-quart or larger electric slow cooker, combine carrots, shallots, and potatoes. Scrub and peel celery root; cut out any dark spots, then cut peeled root into ½-inch cubes and add to potato mixture. In a small bowl, mix broth, lemon juice, and honey; pour over potato mixture. Dot with butter. Cover and cook at low setting until vegetables are very tender when pierced (8 to 10 hours). Season to taste with salt and pepper; sprinkle with parsley. Makes 4 to 6 servings.

Per serving: 150 calories (16% from fat), 3 g protein, 30 g carbohydrates, 3 g total fat (1 g saturated), 6 mg cholesterol, 151 mg sodium

Crockery Ratatouille

Preparation time: About 30 minutes

Cooking time: 6¼ to 8¼ hours

Over hours of slow cooking, the flavors of oven-browned eggplant, tomatoes, sweet red pepper, garlic, and fresh basil blend harmoniously. Shortly before serving, stir in sliced zucchini; just 15 minutes of simmering turn it tender-crisp, without fading its bright color.

      Olive oil cooking spray
   1 **medium-size eggplant (about 1 lb.),
      unpeeled, cut into ½- by 2-inch sticks**
   1½ **pounds pear-shaped (Roma-type) tomatoes,
      seeded and cut into ¼-inch-thick slices**
   1 **large onion, finely chopped**
   1 **medium-size red bell pepper, seeded and
      finely chopped**
   3 **cloves garlic, minced or pressed**
   1 **cup chopped fresh basil or ⅓ cup dry basil**
   ½ **teaspoon** *each* **salt and dry oregano**
   ⅛ **teaspoon pepper**
   ¼ **cup olive oil**
   2 **medium-size zucchini (about 8 oz.** *total***), cut
      into ¼-inch-thick slices**

Spray a large, shallow baking pan with cooking spray. Spread eggplant in pan; spray with cooking spray. Bake in a 425° oven until eggplant is golden brown and soft when pressed (about 25 minutes).

Meanwhile, in a 3½-quart or larger electric slow cooker, combine tomatoes, onion, bell pepper, garlic, basil, salt, oregano, and pepper. Mix in baked eggplant sticks. Drizzle with oil. Cover and cook at low setting until tomatoes have cooked down to form a sauce (6 to 8 hours).

Stir in zucchini. Increase cooker heat setting to high; cover and cook until zucchini is tender-crisp to bite (about 15 more minutes). Makes 6 to 8 servings.

Per serving: 135 calories (54% from fat), 3 g protein, 14 g carbohydrates, 9 g total fat (1 g saturated), 0 mg cholesterol, 170 mg sodium

Red Cabbage with Apricots & Lemon

Preparation time: About 20 minutes

Cooking time: 5½ to 6½ hours

Sweet-sour red cabbage typically gets its tang from sugar and vinegar, but this unusual version of the dish relies instead on honey, dried apricots, red wine, and lemon juice. You might serve it with roast pork or a crisp roast duck.

- **1 head red cabbage (2 to 2½ lbs.), cored and thinly sliced**
- **1 cup chopped dried apricots**
- **¼ cup honey**
- **2 tablespoons lemon juice**
- **½ cup dry red wine**
  Salt

In a 4-quart or larger electric slow cooker, combine cabbage and apricots. In a small bowl, mix honey and lemon juice; drizzle over cabbage mixture. Pour in wine. Cover and cook at low setting until cabbage is very tender to bite (5½ to 6½ hours). Season to taste with salt. Makes 6 servings.

Per serving: 134 calories (3% from fat), 3 g protein, 34 g carbohydrates, 0.5 g total fat (0 g saturated), 0 mg cholesterol, 20 mg sodium

Tarragon Artichokes with Leeks

Preparation time: About 20 minutes

Cooking time: 6¼ to 7¼ hours

Tender quartered artichokes in a creamy, tarragon-seasoned sauce are good with grilled or roasted chicken or veal. In the market, choose very small artichokes—just 2 to 2½ inches in diameter.

- **2 quarts cold water**
- **¼ cup lemon juice**
- **12 small artichokes, *each* 2 to 2½ inches in diameter (2 to 2¼ lbs. *total*)**
- **3 leeks (white and pale green parts only), thinly sliced**
- **¼ cup tarragon vinegar**
- **½ cup dry white wine**
- **1 dry bay leaf**
- **½ teaspoon dry tarragon**
- **⅛ teaspoon *each* ground nutmeg and ground white pepper**
- **1 teaspoon cornstarch**
- **¼ cup whipping cream**
  Salt

In a large bowl, combine cold water and lemon juice; set aside. Using a stainless steel knife, cut stem and top third of leaves from one artichoke, then break off outer leaves until you reach pale green inner ones. Discard outer leaves and trimmings; cut artichoke lengthwise into quarters and immediately drop into lemon water. Repeat to prepare remaining artichokes.

In a 3-quart or larger electric slow cooker, combine leeks, vinegar, wine, bay leaf, tarragon, nutmeg, and white pepper. Drain artichokes, then mix lightly into leek mixture. Cover and cook at low setting until artichokes are very tender when pierced (6 to 7 hours).

In a small bowl, mix cornstarch and cream until smooth; blend into artichoke mixture. Increase cooker heat setting to high; cover and cook, stirring 2 or 3 times, until sauce is thickened (10 to 15 more minutes). Season to taste with salt. Makes 6 servings.

Per serving: 80 calories (33% from fat), 3 g protein, 12 g carbohydrates, 3 g total fat (2 g saturated), 11 mg cholesterol, 70 mg sodium

Wild Rice with Golden Raisins

Preparation time: About 10 minutes

Cooking time: 5½ to 6 hours

Cooking wild rice the usual way takes a fairly long time. Preparing it in a slow cooker takes even longer, but you don't need to watch the pot—and the rice turns out perfectly tender.

  1¾ **cups wild rice**
  ½ **cup golden raisins**
  1 **medium-size onion, finely chopped**
  1 **teaspoon dry thyme**
  5 **cups chicken or beef broth**
  2 **tablespoons dry sherry (optional)**
  3 **tablespoons thinly sliced green onions**

Place rice in a fine wire strainer and rinse under running water. In a 3-quart or larger electric slow cooker, combine rice, raisins, chopped onion, and thyme. Pour in broth. Cover and cook at low setting until broth has been absorbed and rice is tender to bite (5½ to 6 hours). Stir in sherry, if desired. Sprinkle with green onions before serving. Makes 8 to 10 servings.

Per serving: 155 calories (6% from fat), 7 g protein, 31 g carbohydrates, 1 g total fat (0.1 g saturated), 0 mg cholesterol, 552 mg sodium

Pictured on facing page

Yams with Candied Apples & Cranberries

Preparation time: About 25 minutes

Cooking time: 8½ to 10 hours

Colorful and sweetly spiced, this medley of yams, diced apple, and tart cranberries is a great partner for baked ham or roast turkey. Sprinkle the dish with toasted pecans just before serving for a crisp, rich-tasting finishing touch.

  3 **large yams or sweet potatoes (1½ to 2 lbs. *total*), peeled and diced**
  1 **medium-size Golden Delicious apple, peeled, cored, and diced**
  1 **cup fresh or frozen (unthawed) cranberries**
  ¾ **cup firmly packed brown sugar**
  1 **teaspoon ground cinnamon**
  ¼ **teaspoon ground nutmeg**
  ⅓ **cup orange-flavored liqueur or orange juice**
  ½ **cup coarsely chopped pecans**

In a 3-quart or larger electric slow cooker, combine yams and apple; sprinkle with cranberries. In a small bowl, mix sugar, cinnamon, and nutmeg; sprinkle over yam mixture. Drizzle with liqueur. Cover and cook at low setting until yams are very tender when pierced (8½ to 10 hours).

Meanwhile, toast pecans in a wide nonstick frying pan over medium heat until golden brown (5 to 8 minutes), stirring occasionally. Pour out of pan and set aside.

To serve, stir yam mixture lightly, then sprinkle with pecans. Makes 6 to 8 servings.

Per serving: 258 calories (19% from fat), 2 g protein, 52 g carbohydrates, 6 g total fat (0.5 g saturated), 0 mg cholesterol, 18 mg sodium

*Luscious fall flavors blend deliciously in Yams with Candied Apples
& Cranberries (recipe on facing page). Try this tempting casserole as part of a
holiday buffet, with baked ham or roast poultry.*

MINI-POTS FOR HOT DIPS

Not all slow cookers are meant for big things. In addition to standard-size crockery cookers with capacities of 3 quarts or more, you'll find smaller-scale stoneware-lined cookers holding just 2 or 4 cups of food. Intended for heating and serving small quantities, these "mini-pots" are perfect for preparing hot dips.

Almost all of the choices on these two pages are appetizers. Hot Artichoke Dip, accented with chiles and Cheddar, and creamy Bean & Olive Dip are both good with tortilla chips or baked flour tortilla triangles. To complement Warm Crab & Almond Spread, Petite Gouda Fondue with Tomatoes & Basil, and Melted Teleme with Brandy & Lemon, you might offer crisply toasted slices from a French bread baguette.

Our last two recipes are sweet dessert delights. Rocky Road Sundae Sauce turns a plain scoop of ice cream into an extra-special treat; Black & White Chocolate Fondue is a luscious dip for big, ripe strawberries.

Hot Artichoke Dip

Preparation time: About 10 minutes
Cooking time: 45 minutes to 1 hour

1 jar (about 6 oz.) marinated artichoke hearts
2 tablespoons canned diced green chiles
¼ cup mayonnaise
1 cup (about 4 oz.) shredded Cheddar cheese

Drain artichokes, reserving marinade; chop artichokes coarsely. In a 2- or 4-cup electric slow cooker, combine artichokes, chiles, mayonnaise, and cheese. Cover and heat until cheese is melted (45 minutes to 1 hour). Stir gently to mix ingredients, then blend in ½ to 1 tablespoon of the reserved artichoke marinade to give mixture a good dipping consistency. Serve hot. Makes about 1½ cups (4 to 6 servings).

Per serving: 203 calories (81% from fat), 7 g protein, 3 g carbohydrates, 19 g total fat (6 g saturated), 30 mg cholesterol, 399 mg sodium

Warm Crab & Almond Spread

Preparation time: About 10 minutes
Cooking time: 1 to 1½ hours

2 small packages (about 3 oz. each) cream cheese, diced
1½ tablespoons milk
1 green onion, thinly sliced
1 teaspoon prepared horseradish
Pinch of ground white pepper
6 ounces cooked crabmeat, drained and flaked
¼ cup slivered almonds
Salt
Chopped parsley

In a greased 2- or 4-cup electric slow cooker, combine cream cheese and milk. Cover and heat until cheese is melted (30 to 45 minutes). Stir in onion, horseradish, and white pepper. Mix in crab, cover, and heat for 30 to 45 more minutes. Meanwhile, toast almonds in a small nonstick frying pan over medium heat until golden brown (5 to 8 minutes), stirring occasionally. Pour out of pan and set aside.

To serve, season crab mixture to taste with salt; sprinkle with almonds and parsley. Makes about 2 cups (6 to 8 servings).

Per serving: 141 calories (73% from fat), 8 g protein, 2 g carbohydrates, 12 g total fat (6 g saturated), 51 mg cholesterol, 143 mg sodium

Bean & Olive Dip

Preparation time: About 10 minutes
Cooking time: 45 minutes to 1 hour

1 small can (about 7 oz.) chili with beans
1 small package (about 3 oz.) cream cheese, diced
¼ cup sliced ripe olives
2 tablespoons canned diced green chiles
Sliced green onions

In a 2- or 4-cup electric slow cooker, combine chili, cream cheese, olives, and chiles. Cover and heat until cheese is melted (45 minutes to 1 hour). Stir gently to mix ingredients. Sprinkle with onions. Makes about 1¾ cups (6 to 8 servings).

Per serving: 80 calories (68% from fat), 3 g protein, 4 g carbohydrates, 6 g total fat (3 g saturated), 18 mg cholesterol, 241 mg sodium

Melted Teleme with Brandy & Lemon

Preparation time: About 10 minutes
Cooking time: 40 to 45 minutes

8 ounces teleme cheese, diced
½ teaspoon coarsely ground pepper
¼ teaspoon grated lemon peel
2 tablespoons brandy
Lemon wedges

Place cheese in a 2- or 4-cup electric slow cooker. Sprinkle with pepper and lemon peel. Cover and heat until cheese is melted (40 to 45 minutes; cheese cubes will hold their shape, but will be soft enough to blend together when stirred). Stir gently to mix.

In a small pan, heat brandy over low heat until warm to the touch. Ignite brandy (not beneath a fan or near flammable items); pour over cheese in cooker. After flames subside, stir again to blend in brandy. Serve with lemon wedges to squeeze over each serving to taste. Makes 6 to 8 servings.

Per serving: 99 calories (68% from fat), 6 g protein, 1 g carbohydrates, 7 g total fat*, 6 mg cholesterol, 171 mg sodium

Petite Gouda Fondue with Tomatoes & Basil

Preparation time: About 15 minutes
Cooking time: 35 to 45 minutes

1 small whole Gouda cheese (about 7 oz.)
2 small pear-shaped (Roma-type) tomatoes, seeded and finely chopped
1 tablespoon finely chopped fresh basil

Remove and discard hard coating from cheese. Using a grapefruit knife, care-

* Data on saturated fat not available

fully scoop out center of cheese, leaving a ¼-inch-thick shell; set shell aside. Cut cheese into ½-inch cubes.

In a 2- or 4-cup electric slow cooker, combine cheese cubes, tomatoes, and basil. Cover and heat until cheese is melted (35 to 45 minutes; cheese cubes will hold their shape, but will be soft enough to blend together when stirred). Stir gently to mix ingredients.

To serve, spoon cheese mixture into cheese shell, pushing out edges to fill shell completely. Serve hot. Makes 6 servings.

Per serving: 122 calories (67% from fat), 8 g protein, 2 g carbohydrates, 9 g total fat (6 g saturated), 38 mg cholesterol, 272 mg sodium

Rocky Road Sundae Sauce

Preparation time: About 5 minutes
Cooking time: 40 to 45 minutes

⅓ cup whipping cream
½ cup miniature marshmallows
1 cup (6 oz.) semisweet chocolate chips
¼ cup slivered almonds
Vanilla or chocolate ice cream

In a 2- or 4-cup electric slow cooker, combine cream, marshmallows, and chocolate chips. Cover and heat until chocolate is melted (40 to 45 minutes). Meanwhile, toast almonds in a small nonstick frying pan over medium heat

until golden brown (5 to 8 minutes), stirring occasionally; pour out of pan and set aside.

Stir chocolate mixture until smooth; then stir in almonds. Spoon hot sauce over ice cream. Makes 6 servings.

Per serving: 217 calories (56% from fat), 3 g protein, 23 g carbohydrates, 15 g total fat (7 g saturated), 15 mg cholesterol, 7 g sodium

Black & White Chocolate Fondue

Preparation time: About 10 minutes
Cooking time: 30 to 45 minutes

4 ounces semisweet chocolate, coarsely chopped
⅓ cup whipping cream
1 tablespoon crème de cacao or brandy
1 ounce white chocolate, coarsely shredded
3 to 4 cups strawberries, rinsed and patted dry

In a 2- or 4-cup electric slow cooker, combine semisweet chocolate and cream. Cover and heat until chocolate is melted (30 to 45 minutes). Stir mixture until smooth. Blend in crème de cacao. Sprinkle white chocolate over surface of fondue, then draw a spoon through fondue 2 or 3 times to swirl white chocolate through. Serve fondue hot, with strawberries for dipping. Makes 4 to 6 servings.

Per serving: 232 calories (55% from fat), 2 g protein, 25 g carbohydrates, 15 g total fat (8 g saturated), 18 mg cholesterol, 11 mg sodium

Slow-cooked with vegetables and prosciutto, savory Herbed Tuscan White Beans & Tomatoes (recipe on facing page) are a wonderful Italian-style partner for grilled sausages, other meats, or poultry. You can make the dish with cannellini (white kidney beans), as shown above— but Great Northern beans are also good.

Potato, Onion & Tomato Gratin

Preparation time: About 25 minutes

Cooking time: 7½ to 8½ hours

Here's a savory side dish from the south of France. Combine thinly sliced potatoes, onion, and Roma tomatoes in your slow cooker; as the tomatoes soften and cook down, the other vegetables simmer to tenderness in the herb-infused juices.

Olive oil cooking spray

1½ to 1¾ pounds russet potatoes, peeled and thinly sliced

6 cloves garlic, minced or pressed

2 tablespoons dry thyme

Salt and freshly ground pepper

1 large onion, thinly sliced

12 ounces pear-shaped (Roma-type) tomatoes, seeded and sliced

2 tablespoons olive oil

3 tablespoons dry white wine

Spray a 3-quart or larger electric slow cooker with cooking spray. Spread about a third of the potatoes in cooker; sprinkle with a third each of the garlic and thyme, then season to taste with salt and pepper. Add a third each of the onion and tomato slices. Repeat layers, using a third of the potatoes, onion, and tomatoes for each layer and seasoning each layer of potatoes with garlic, thyme, salt, and pepper; finish with a tomato layer. Drizzle with oil and wine. Cover and cook at low setting until potatoes in center of mixture are very tender when pierced (7½ to 8½ hours). Makes 6 to 8 servings.

Per serving: 126 calories (32% from fat), 3 g protein, 20 g carbohydrates, 5 g total fat (1 g saturated), 0 mg cholesterol, 11 mg sodium

Pictured on facing page

Herbed Tuscan White Beans & Tomatoes

Preparation time: About 1 hour (including standing time)

Cooking time: 9½ to 10½ hours

To make this robustly seasoned dish, you can use either dried cannellini (white kidney beans) or the more familiar Great Northern beans. (Stores specializing in Italian foods often sell cannellini in bulk.)

1 pound dried cannellini (white kidney beans) or Great Northern beans

2 quarts water

1 medium-size onion, thinly sliced

2 leeks (white and pale green parts only), thinly sliced

3 cloves garlic, minced or pressed

1 medium-size carrot, shredded

4 ounces prosciutto, chopped

1 tablespoon dry sage

½ teaspoon *each* dry rosemary and pepper

¼ teaspoon baking soda

2 tablespoons olive oil

1 can (about 14½ oz.) chicken broth

4 pear-shaped (Roma-type) tomatoes, seeded and chopped

2 tablespoons balsamic vinegar

Salt

Italian parsley leaves

Rinse and sort through beans. In a deep 3½- to 4-quart pan, bring water to a boil over high heat. Add beans. Let water return to a boil; then boil, uncovered, for 2 minutes. Remove pan from heat, cover, and let stand for 1 hour. Drain and rinse beans, discarding cooking water.

While beans are standing, in a 3½-quart or larger electric slow cooker, combine onion, leeks, garlic, carrot, prosciutto, sage, rosemary, pepper, and baking soda. Add beans to cooker, then pour in oil and broth. Cover and cook at low setting until beans are very tender to bite (9 to 10 hours); if possible, stir once during last hour of cooking.

Gently stir in tomatoes and vinegar. Increase cooker heat setting to high; cover and cook until tomatoes are hot (about 30 more minutes). Season to taste with salt and garnish with parsley. Makes 8 servings.

Per serving: 278 calories (18% from fat), 17 g protein, 41 g carbohydrates, 6 g total fat (1 g saturated), 8 mg cholesterol, 478 mg sodium

Warm Lentil Salad

Preparation time: About 15 minutes
Cooking time: 6 to 7 hours

Scooped into crisp radicchio or butter lettuce cups, this tangy lentil salad is a pleasing accompaniment for roast chicken or grilled lamb.

- 1½ cups lentils, rinsed and drained
- ½ cup chopped Black Forest or Westphalian ham
- 1 medium-size onion, thinly sliced
- 1 clove garlic, minced or pressed
- 1 dry bay leaf
- ¼ teaspoon *each* dry rosemary and pepper
- 3 cups water
- 2 tablespoons olive oil
- ⅓ cup *each* red wine vinegar and chopped parsley
  Salt
  Radicchio or butter lettuce leaves, rinsed and crisped

In a 3-quart or larger electric slow cooker, combine lentils, ham, onion, garlic, bay leaf, rosemary, and pepper. Pour in water. Cover and cook at low setting until lentils are tender when mashed with a fork (6 to 7 hours). Drain lentil mixture, if necessary; remove and discard bay leaf. Mix in oil, vinegar, and parsley; season to taste with salt.

To serve, arrange radicchio leaves on individual salad plates; spoon warm lentil mixture into leaves. Makes 6 servings.

Per serving: 228 calories (22% from fat), 16 g protein, 30 g carbohydrates, 6 g total fat (1 g saturated), 6 mg cholesterol, 147 mg sodium

Western-style Bean Pot

Preparation time: About 1 hour (including standing time)
Cooking time: 10¼ to 12¼ hours

Southwestern seasonings and the use of two kinds of beans—pinto and small white—distinguish this otherwise traditional recipe. Flavored by a meaty ham hock, the slowly simmered beans are a good choice for a buffet or picnic.

- 8 ounces dried pinto beans
- 8 ounces dried small white or Great Northern beans
- 2 quarts plus 1 cup water
- 1 medium-size onion, thinly sliced
- 1 smoked ham hock (about 1 lb.)
- ½ cup light molasses
- ¼ cup firmly packed brown sugar
- 1 tablespoon *each* dry mustard and chili powder
- ¾ teaspoon salt
- ¼ teaspoon baking soda
- 1 teaspoon ground cumin
- 1 can or bottle (about 12 oz.) beer
- ¼ cup catsup

Rinse and sort through beans. In a deep 3½- to 4-quart pan, bring 2 quarts of the water to a boil over high heat. Add beans. Let water return to a boil; then boil, uncovered, for 2 minutes. Remove pan from heat, cover, and let stand for 1 hour. Drain and rinse beans, discarding cooking water.

While beans are standing, in a 3-quart or larger electric slow cooker, combine onion and ham hock. In a small bowl, mix molasses, sugar, mustard, chili powder, salt, baking soda, and cumin; set aside. Add beans to cooker; spoon molasses mixture over beans. Pour in beer, then remaining 1 cup water. Cover and cook at low setting until beans are very tender to bite (10 to 12 hours).

Lift out ham hock and let stand until cool enough to handle. Meanwhile, mix catsup into beans and increase cooker heat setting to high. Remove and discard fat and bone from ham; tear meat into bite-size pieces and stir into beans. Cover; cook until ham is heated through (about 15 more minutes). Makes 8 servings.

Per serving: 320 calories (6% from fat), 16 g protein, 61 g carbohydrates, 2 g total fat (0 g saturated), 9 mg cholesterol, 612 mg sodium

Coconut Red Beans & Rice

Preparation time: About 1 hour (including standing time)

Cooking time: 8¾ to 10¾ hours

Time-honored partners, beans and rice dance to a Caribbean beat when they're cooked with coconut milk and a hint of chile. Serve this dish as a hearty complement to grilled chicken breasts; to round out the meal, you might warm up some lime-basted pineapple or papaya wedges on the barbecue alongside the chicken.

- 1 **cup dried small red beans**
- 2 **quarts water**
- 1 **large onion, finely chopped**
- 2 **cloves garlic, minced or pressed**
- ⅛ **teaspoon baking soda**
- 1 **small dried hot red chile**
- 1 **can (12 to 14 oz.) coconut milk, thawed if frozen**
- 3 **cups chicken broth or water**
- 1½ **cups long-grain white rice**
  Salt
  Lime wedges

Rinse and sort through beans. In a deep 3½- to 4-quart pan, bring the 2 quarts water to a boil over high heat. Add beans. Let water return to a boil; then boil, uncovered, for 2 minutes. Remove pan from heat, cover, and let stand for 1 hour. Drain and rinse beans, discarding cooking water.

While beans are standing, in a 3½-quart or larger electric slow cooker, combine onion, garlic, baking soda, chile, and coconut milk. Add beans to cooker; pour in broth. Cover; cook at low setting until beans are very tender to bite (8 to 10 hours).

Remove and discard chile from beans; mix in rice. Increase cooker heat setting to high; cover and cook until rice is tender to bite (35 to 40 minutes). Season to taste with salt; offer lime wedges to squeeze over each serving to taste. Makes 8 to 10 servings.

Per serving: 283 calories (30% from fat), 9 g protein, 42 g carbohydrates, 10 g total fat (8 g saturated), 0 mg cholesterol, 350 mg sodium

Spoonbread with Roasted Garlic

Preparation time: About 30 minutes

Cooking time: 2½ to 3 hours

Flavored with sweet roasted garlic, this moist and savory cornmeal pudding is an excellent accompaniment for grilled or sautéed pork chops.

- 1 **tablespoon olive oil**
- 1 **head garlic, cut in half crosswise**
- ¾ **cup yellow cornmeal**
- 2 **teaspoons sugar**
- ¼ **teaspoon *each* salt and ground red pepper (cayenne)**
- 2 **cups milk**
- 2 **tablespoons butter or margarine**
- 4 **eggs, separated**
- ¼ **cup grated Parmesan cheese**

Pour oil into a small baking pan; place garlic, cut sides down, in pan. Bake in a 375° oven until garlic is golden brown on bottom (20 to 25 minutes). Let garlic stand until cool enough to handle; squeeze garlic from skins into a medium-size bowl. Mash garlic coarsely with a fork and set aside.

While garlic is baking, in a 3- to 4-quart pan, stir together cornmeal, sugar, salt, and red pepper. Using a wire whisk, blend in milk; add butter. Place over medium-high heat and cook, whisking constantly, until mixture boils and thickens (3 to 5 minutes). Remove from heat and let cool slightly.

Beat egg yolks into garlic. Stir a little of the hot cornmeal mixture into egg yolk mixture, then blend yolk mixture into cornmeal mixture in pan. Stir in cheese. In a large bowl, beat egg whites until stiff but not dry. Gently fold egg whites into cornmeal mixture. Pour into a greased 3- to 4-quart electric slow cooker. Cover and cook at low setting until spoonbread looks dry on top and a skewer inserted in center comes out clean (2½ to 3 hours). Makes 4 to 6 servings.

Per serving: 306 calories (48% from fat), 13 g protein, 28 g carbohydrates, 16 g total fat (7 g saturated), 199 mg cholesterol, 331 mg sodium

Toasted Corn Pudding

Preparation time: About 25 minutes

Cooking time: 2¾ to 3½ hours

Tender fresh corn kernels, lightly toasted before being cut from the cobs, add sweetness to this spicy vegetable pudding. Squares of the tangy custard are good with summer barbecue fare—such as chicken, lamb, or spareribs—and a big, leafy salad.

     3 **ears corn, husks and silk removed**
     2 **tablespoons butter or margarine**
     4 **ounces soft goat cheese or cream cheese**
     ¼ **cup canned diced green chiles**
     3 **tablespoons all-purpose flour**
     ⅛ **teaspoon ground red pepper (cayenne)**
     ¼ **teaspoon salt**
   1½ **cups lowfat milk**
     3 **eggs**
        Paprika
        Cilantro sprigs (optional)

In a wide nonstick frying pan, toast corn ears over medium heat, turning as needed, until about a third of the kernels on each ear are tinged with brown (about 15 minutes). Remove from pan; let stand until cool enough to handle. Cut kernels from ears and return to pan. Add butter and cheese; stir over medium heat until butter and cheese are melted. Stir in chiles. Remove pan from heat; sprinkle corn mixture with flour, red pepper, and salt, then stir lightly to blend.

Spoon corn mixture into a greased 3- to 4-quart electric slow cooker. In a bowl, beat milk and eggs until blended; pour over corn mixture. Sprinkle lightly with paprika. Cover and cook at low setting until a knife inserted in center of pudding comes out clean (2¾ to 3½ hours). Let stand for about 5 minutes, then cut into pieces to serve. Garnish with cilantro sprigs, if desired. Makes 8 servings.

Per serving: 158 calories (52% from fat), 8 g protein, 12 g carbohydrates, 9 g total fat (3 g saturated), 91 mg cholesterol, 314 mg sodium

Saucy All-day Apples

Preparation time: About 20 minutes

Cooking time: 6½ to 8 hours

As the slow cooker's gentle heat turns sliced apples into spicy sauce, an irresistible aroma fills the air. Serve the applesauce warm with roast pork, or spoon it over hot gingerbread for an easy dessert.

   2½ **pounds medium-size Golden Delicious apples, peeled, cored, and cut into ½-inch-thick slices**
     ⅓ **cup sugar**
     1 **cinnamon stick (about 2 inches long)**
     2 **tablespoons lemon juice**
        Freshly ground nutmeg

Spread apple slices in a 3-quart or larger electric slow cooker. Sprinkle with sugar; insert cinnamon stick down between apples. Drizzle with lemon juice. Cover and cook at low setting until apples form a thick sauce (6½ to 8 hours).

Remove and discard cinnamon stick. Sprinkle with nutmeg; serve warm or at room temperature. Makes 6 servings.

Per serving: 131 calories (3% from fat), 0.2 g protein, 34 g carbohydrates, 0.5 g total fat (0.1 g saturated), 0 mg cholesterol, 1 mg sodium

Even when it's too hot to bake, you can enjoy our Toasted
Corn Pudding (recipe on facing page), made with fresh sweet corn. Cut it into
squares to serve with herb-strewn grilled or broiled Cornish hens
and tomato halves.

LEISURELY DESSERTS

For poaching fruits or preparing the warm, homey puddings reminiscent of more leisurely times, the crockery cooker is an ideal choice. Our dessert sampler begins with dramatic orange-sauced Pears Fandango; for delicious contrast, top the hot fruit with cooling dollops of softly whipped cream.

You'll also want to try cozy Spicy Rice Pudding, flavored with cinnamon and a sophisticated touch of marsala wine; brandied Apple-Pecan Bread Pudding; and Maple-Spice Indian Pudding. Or transform your slow cooker into a steamer by placing a small round rack inside, then prepare delectable Steamed Cocoa Pudding. All four puddings are especially inviting when served with a scoop of vanilla ice cream or a drizzling of whipping cream.

Pictured on page 94

Pears Fandango

Preparation time: About 20 minutes
Cooking time: 5¾ to 6¾ hours

½ cup firmly packed brown sugar
½ teaspoon ground cinnamon
2 tablespoons finely chopped crystallized ginger
6 medium-size Bosc or Anjou pears
¼ cup orange-flavored liqueur or orange juice
2 tablespoons lemon juice
1 teaspoon grated lemon peel
1 tablespoon butter or margarine
1½ teaspoons cornstarch blended with 1 tablespoon cold water

Orange and lemon slices
Mint sprigs
Softly whipped cream (optional)

In a deep 3½-quart or larger electric slow cooker, mix sugar, cinnamon, and ginger. Peel pears; then core, starting from blossom ends and leaving stems attached. Stand pears upright in cooker on top of sugar mixture (if necessary, trim bases so pears stand upright). In a small bowl, mix liqueur, lemon juice, and lemon peel; pour over pears. Dot with butter. Cover and cook at low setting until pears are tender when pierced (5½ to 6½ hours).

Carefully lift out pears and stand upright in a shallow bowl. Blend cornstarch mixture into cooking liquid. Increase cooker heat setting to high; cover and cook, stirring once or twice, until sauce is thickened (about 10 more min-

utes). Spoon sauce over pears. Garnish with orange and lemon slices and mint sprigs. Serve with whipped cream, if desired. Makes 6 servings.

Per serving: 218 calories (10% from fat), 1 g protein, 52 g carbohydrates, 3 g total fat (1 g saturated), 5 mg cholesterol, 29 mg sodium

Maple-Spice Indian Pudding

Preparation time: About 20 minutes
Cooking time: 8 to 9 hours

¼ cup light molasses
½ cup maple syrup
4 cups milk
⅔ cup yellow cornmeal
⅓ cup sugar
½ teaspoon salt
1 teaspoon ground cinnamon
½ teaspoon ground nutmeg
¼ teaspoon ground ginger
2 tablespoons butter or margarine
Whipped cream or vanilla ice cream (optional)

In a heavy medium-size pan, combine molasses, syrup, and 3 cups of the milk. Place over medium heat and cook, stirring occasionally, until mixture is steaming (8 to 10 minutes); do not boil. Meanwhile, in a small bowl, mix cornmeal, sugar, salt, cinnamon, nutmeg, and ginger. Stir cornmeal mixture into milk mixture; reduce heat to low. Cook, stirring often, until mixture thickens and bubbles vigorously (6 to 8 minutes). Stir in butter.

Pour cornmeal mixture into a greased 3- to 4-quart electric slow cooker; then pour remaining 1 cup milk over cornmeal mixture. Cover and cook at low setting until pudding is shiny on top and set in center (8 to 9 hours). Serve with whipped cream or ice cream, if desired. Makes 6 to 8 servings.

Per serving: 287 calories (25% from fat), 6 g protein, 49 g carbohydrates, 8 g total fat (5 g saturated), 28 mg cholesterol, 263 mg sodium

Steamed Cocoa Pudding

Preparation time: About 20 minutes
Cooking time: 1½ to 2 hours

¾ **cup all-purpose flour**
¼ **cup unsweetened cocoa**
2 **teaspoons baking powder**
2 **eggs, separated**
1 **cup sugar**
¼ **cup butter or margarine, at room temperature**
½ **cup Irish cream liqueur; or ½ cup whipping cream mixed with 1 teaspoon brandy flavoring**
½ **cup coffee-flavored yogurt**
Whipped cream (optional)

In a small bowl, stir together flour, cocoa, and baking powder; set aside. In a large bowl, beat egg whites with an electric mixer until foamy. Gradually add ¼ cup of the sugar, beating until mixture holds soft peaks; set aside.

In another large bowl, combine butter and remaining ¾ cup sugar; beat until well combined. Beat in egg yolks, one at a time. Gradually blend in half the flour mixture. Add liqueur; beat just until blended. Blend in remaining flour mixture. Add yogurt; beat just to blend. Lightly fold in egg whites. Transfer mixture to a greased 1½- to 2-quart soufflé dish; cover tightly with foil.

Place a rack in a 4-quart or larger electric slow cooker; pour in hot water to a depth of 1 inch (don't worry if water comes above rack). Place soufflé dish on rack. Cover and cook at high

setting until pudding feels firm when lightly touched and a wooden pick inserted in center comes out clean (1½ to 2 hours). Serve pudding warm, with whipped cream, if desired. Makes 6 to 8 servings.

Per serving: 309 calories (34% from fat), 5 g protein, 46 g carbohydrates, 12 g total fat (7 g saturated), 89 mg cholesterol, 221 mg sodium

Spicy Rice Pudding

Preparation time: About 10 minutes
Cooking time: 7 to 8 hours

3 **cups milk**
½ **cup raisins**
⅓ **cup short-grain white rice**
¼ **cup sugar**
1 **cinnamon stick (about 2 inches long)**
½ **teaspoon vanilla**
2 **tablespoons dry or sweet marsala**
⅓ **cup whipping cream**
Freshly ground nutmeg

In a greased 3-quart or larger electric slow cooker, combine milk, raisins, rice, sugar, cinnamon stick, and vanilla. Cover and cook at low setting until pudding is thick and creamy and rice is tender to bite (7 to 8 hours).

Remove liner from cooker (if using a cooker with a fixed liner, turn heat off and let pudding stand for about 10 minutes before continuing). Remove and discard cinnamon stick. Stir marsala into pudding. In a small bowl, beat cream until stiff; fold into pudding. Transfer to a serving bowl, if desired. Sprinkle with nutmeg. Makes 4 to 6 servings.

Per serving: 276 calories (32% from fat), 6 g protein, 40 g carbohydrates, 10 g total fat (6 g saturated), 38 mg cholesterol, 79 mg sodium

Apple-Pecan Bread Pudding

Preparation time: About 20 minutes
Cooking time: 3½ to 4½ hours

1 **cup coarsely chopped pecans**
8 **slices raisin bread, diced**
2 **medium-size tart green apples**
1 **cup sugar**
1 **teaspoon ground cinnamon**
½ **teaspoon ground nutmeg**
3 **eggs**
2 **cups half-and-half**
¼ **cup bourbon or brandy**
¼ **cup butter or margarine, melted**
Vanilla ice cream (optional)

Spread pecans in a shallow baking pan. Bake in a 350° oven until golden brown (8 to 10 minutes), stirring occasionally.

Meanwhile, place bread cubes in a greased 3-quart or larger electric slow cooker. Peel, core, and thinly slice apples; mix lightly with bread. In a large bowl, stir together sugar, cinnamon, and nutmeg; add eggs and mix well. Blend in half-and-half, then stir in bourbon.

Lightly mix pecans with bread mixture; pour egg mixture over bread. Drizzle with butter. Cover; cook at low setting until apples are tender when pierced and custard is set (3½ to 4½ hours). Let pudding stand, covered, for about 15 minutes; then serve warm, with ice cream, if desired. Makes 8 to 10 servings.

Per serving: 383 calories (50% from fat), 6 g protein, 44 g carbohydrates, 22 g total fat (8 g saturated), 105 mg cholesterol, 176 mg sodium

The remarkable slow cooker can even turn out tempting desserts!
Pears Fandango (recipe on page 92) poach to tenderness in a sweet, spicy
brown sugar sauce that's accented with orange and lemon. Serve
the fruit warm, with softly whipped cream.

Index